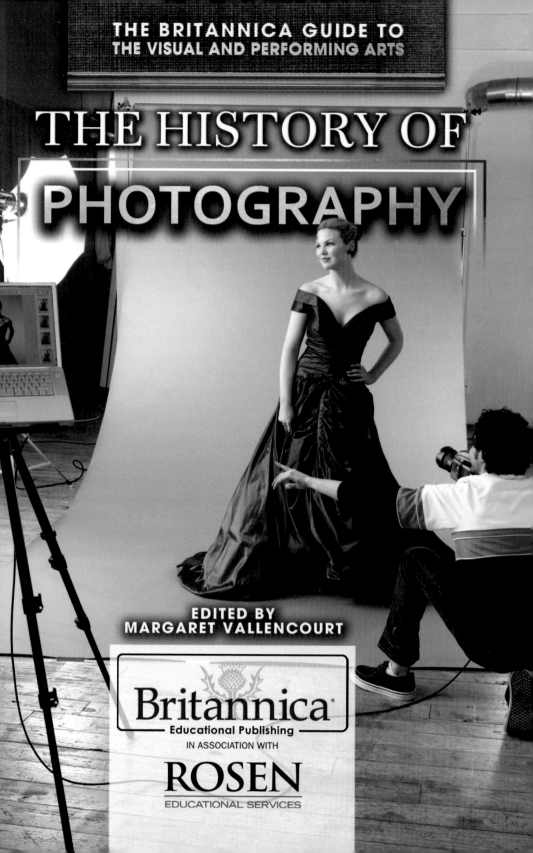

THE BRITANNICA GUIDE TO
THE VISUAL AND PERFORMING ARTS

THE HISTORY OF
PHOTOGRAPHY

EDITED BY
MARGARET VALLENCOURT

Britannica
Educational Publishing
IN ASSOCIATION WITH

ROSEN
EDUCATIONAL SERVICES

Published in 2016 by Britannica Educational Publishing (a trademark of Ency-clopædia Britannica, Inc.) in association with The Rosen Publishing Group, Inc. 29 East 21st Street, New York, NY 10010

Distributed exclusively by Rosen Publishing.
To see additional Britannica Educational Publishing titles, go to rosenpublishing.com.

First Edition

Britannica Educational Publishing
J.E. Luebering: Director, Core Reference Group
Anthony L. Green: Editor, Compton's by Britannica

Rosen Publishing
Hope Lourie Killcoyne: Executive Editor
Christine Poolos: Editor
Nelson Sá: Art Director
Nicole Russo: Designer
Cindy Reiman: Photography Manager

Library of Congress Cataloging-in-Publication Data

The history of photography/edited by Margaret Vallencourt.—First edition.
    pages cm.—(The Britannica guide to the visual and performing arts)
Includes bibliographical references and index.
ISBN 978-1-68048-073-3 (library bound)
1. Photography—History—Juvenile literature. I. Vallencourt, Margaret, editor.
TR149.H56 2016
770.9—dc23

2014039882

Manufactured in the United States of America

Photo credits: Cover, p. i Ryan McVay/The Image Bank/Getty Images; pp. xi, 137, 146, 154 © AP Images; p. xvi Edward Steichen/The Life Picture Collection/Getty Images; p. xxi Larry Burrows/The Life Picture Collection/ Getty Images; p. 2 © Photos.com/Jupiterimages; p. 7 Collection de la Société Françaiçe de Photographie, Paris; p. 11 The Mansell Collection/Art Resource, NY; p. 21 Science & Society Picture Library/Getty Images; pp. 29, 35, 42, 56, 75, 93 Library of Congress Prints and Photographs Division; p. 39 Courtesy of the Caisse Nationale des Monuments Historiques, Paris; pp. 48, 61, 95, 119, 165 Library of Congress, Washington, D.C.; p. 68 Royal Photographic Society/SSPL/Getty Images; p. 80 © 1971, Aperture Foundation, Inc., Paul Strand Archive; p. 84 © Edward Weston; p. 99 Universal History Archive/UIG/Getty Images; p. 101 Oli Scarff/Getty Images; p. 107 W. Eugene Smith/The Life Picture Collection/Getty Images; p. 131 Anthony Barboza/Archive Photos/ Getty Images; p. 142 Roz Kelly/Michael Ochs Archives/Getty Images; p. 152 Hulton Archive/Getty Images; p. 179 Getty Images; cover and interior pages graphic elements David M. Schrader/Shutterstock.com, E_K/Shutterstock.com, Valentin Agapov/Shutterstock.com, argus/Shutterstock.com, Iakov Filimonov/ Shutterstock.com.

CONTENTS

CHAPTER 4
CONTEMPORARY PHOTOGRAPHY: 1945–PRESENT

The word "photography" comes from two ancient Greek words: *photo*, for "light," and *graph*, for "drawing." "Drawing with light" is a way of describing photography. When a photograph is made, light or some other form of radiant energy, such as X-rays, is used to record a picture of an object or scene on a light-sensitive surface. Early photographs were called sun pictures, because sunlight itself was used to create the image.

Humans have been creating images at least since cave paintings of some 20,000 years ago. With the invention of photography, a realistic image that would have taken a skilled artist hours or even days to draw could be recorded in exact detail within a fraction of a second. Today, photography has become a powerful means of communication and a mode of visual expression that touches human life in many ways. For example, photography has become popular as a means of crystallizing memories.

Most of the billions of photographs taken today are casual records to document personal events such as vacations, birthdays, and weddings. Photographs are used extensively by newspapers, magazines, books, and television to convey information and advertise products and services.

Practical applications of photography are found in nearly every human endeavor from astronomy to medical diagnosis to industrial quality control. Photography extends human vision into the realm of objects that are invisible because they are too small or too distant, or events that occur too rapidly for the naked eye to detect. A camera can be used in locations too dangerous for humans. Photographs can also be objects of art that explore the human condition and provide aesthetic pleasure. And for many, photography is a satisfying hobby or a rewarding career.

PHOTOGRAPHY IN COMMUNICATION

Since its invention in 1839, photography's unique powers of visual description have been used to record, report, and inform. People prefer to see things with their own eyes, but when this is impossible the camera can often serve the same purpose almost as well. It is not true that photographs never lie—they can be falsified and manipulated. Nevertheless, a photograph can carry a strong measure of authenticity and conviction. As a nonverbal means of communication, photography can surmount the barriers of language and communicate through universal visual symbols.

Photographs are well suited for use in the mass media. Today they are reproduced by the billions, and they can be found everywhere: in the pages of newspapers, magazines, books, catalogs, and brochures; on display in billboards, shop windows, and posters; broadcast over television; and organized into slide shows and film strips.

In photography's early days some of its most eagerly sought images were those brought back by explorers and travelers. These

Photojournalists capture images of events and places that most people cannot access, such as this Joel Meyerowitz photo of Ground Zero following the 9/11 attacks.

would satisfy people's curiosity about distant places like China, Egypt, and the American West. That same kind of curiosity exists today. People are fascinated with photographs of the surface of the moon, the landscape of Mars, and the appearance of other planets in the solar system.

Photographs in the mass-communication media have made the faces of political leaders, popular entertainers, and other celebrities familiar to the public. When a newsworthy event occurs, photojournalists are there to record it. Photojournalists sometimes spend months covering a story. The result of such labor is often a powerful, revealing picture essay that probes far beneath the surface of events.

Photography is also essential to the advertising industry. In efforts to sell a product, attractive photographs of the item are used. Photography is also widely used in education and training within the academic world, industry, and the armed services.

Photographs are also often used in attempts to sway public opinion. Governments, political parties, and special-interest groups have long used the graphic representation and emotional impact of photographs to further their causes. Such use may result in destructive propaganda, such as that of the Nazis during the Third Reich. Significant changes have been brought about by way of photography. Photographs of the Yellowstone region, for example, were instrumental in Congress's decision to establish that area as a national park in 1872; and photographs of child laborers helped to bring about legislation protecting children from exploitation as early as 1916.

PHOTOGRAPHY IN SCIENCE AND TECHNOLOGY

Photography has many practical applications in industry, medicine, astronomy, archaeology, scientific research, the graphic arts, law enforcement, and many aspects of contemporary life. Aerial photography, for example, is used to make maps and contour charts, to study the Earth and its oceans, and to help forecast the weather. Cameras aboard satellites and space vehicles have photographed the Earth, as well as the moon, the sun, and the other planets. Astronomers use photography to study galaxies in deep space and to analyze the composition of stars through spectroscopy. New photographic applications are constantly being developed.

Industrial and scientific researchers rely heavily on photography. For example, objects too small to be seen with the naked eye can be clearly recorded in photomicrographs—

photographic images made through optical or electron microscopes. Ultra-high-speed electronic flash photography can record events that happen too fast to be seen by the unaided eye. With exposures as brief as one-millionth of a second, an electronic-flash photograph can "freeze" a bullet traveling at 15,000 miles per hour (24,000 kilometers per hour).

Photography is used extensively in medicine and dentistry for research, teaching, and as a day-to-day diagnostic tool. Especially important are films made with X-rays, which reveal the body's inner structure.

The world of miniaturized electronic equipment would not be possible without photography. A photographic etching process called photoresist is used to produce the extremely small but precisely printed microelectronic chips that are the "brains" of modern electronic hardware.

Photography by ultraviolet light has a number of applications, including the detection of forged or altered documents, the identification of chemical compounds, and the examination of bacterial colonies. Infrared photography can, in effect, "see in the dark." It can record invisible infrared illumination. It has significant military and surveillance uses and is also employed in medical and astronomical photography.

PHOTOGRAPHY AS ART

Today photography is widely recognized as a fine art. Photographs are displayed in art museums, prized by collectors, discussed by critics, and studied in art history courses. Because of the special nature of photography, however, this was not always the case. In the early days of photography some people considered the medium something of a poor relation to the older, established visual arts, such as drawing and painting.

The arguments stemmed from the fact that a camera is a mechanical instrument. Because the mechanical procedure of taking a picture is automatic, detractors claimed that photography required no coordination of hand and eye and none of the manual skills essential to drawing and painting. They also argued that photography required no creativity or imagination because the photographic subject was "ready-made" and did not require manipulation or control by the photographer.

A camera, no matter how many automatic features it may have, is a lifeless piece of equipment until a person uses it. It then becomes a uniquely responsive tool—an extension of the photographer's eye and mind. A photographer creates a picture by a process of selection. Photographers looking through the camera's viewfinder must decide what to

Edward Steichen captured the melancholy and the mystery of the city when he photographed New York City's Flatiron Building in 1909.

include and what to exclude from the scene. They select the distance from which to take the picture and the precise angle that best suits their purpose. They select the instant in which to trip the shutter. This decision may require hours of patient waiting until the light is exactly right or it may be a split-second decision, but the photographer's sense of timing is always crucial.

Photographers can expand or flatten perspective by the use of certain lenses. They can freeze motion or record it as a blur, depending on their choice of shutter speed. They can create an infinite number of lighting effects with flashes or floodlights. They can alter the tonal values or colours in a picture by their choice of film and filters. These are only a few of the controls available to a photographer when taking a picture. Later, in the darkroom, many additional choices are available.

One of the best ways to view artistic photographs is to visit museums. Today most art museums include photography exhibitions, and many have a photography department and a permanent collection of photographic prints. This is a relatively recent development. The first international exhibition of artistic photography took place in Vienna, Austria, in 1891, and in 1910 the Albright Gallery in Buffalo, New York, held a large exhibition of work by contemporary photographers. This exhibition was sponsored by a group of photographers, including Alfred Stieglitz and Edward Steichen, known as the Photo-Secession group. It was not until 1940, however, that a museum—the Museum of Modern Art in New York City—established a separate department of photography. In 1992 the Metropolitan Museum of Art in New York City created a department devoted solely to photography. The International Museum of Photography at George Eastman House in Rochester, New York, has one of the world's greatest historical collections. In Washington, D.C., the Library of Congress, the National Archives, and the Smithsonian Institution also house extensive photographic collections.

Today photography collections exist in art museums throughout the world and in some colleges and universities. Founded in 1974, the International Center of Photography in New York City contains a museum, school, and research center. Chicago's Museum of Contemporary Photography is the Midwest's greatest repository of photography and an active supporter of working photographers. There has also been a growth of photographic galleries and art galleries that maintain a photographic department. Major events for collectors, gallery owners, and art dealers are the auctions held periodically by major art dealers. Here, rare or sought-after photographs may command thousands of dollars.

THE HOBBY OF PHOTOGRAPHY

Taking photographs is a popular activity. The invention and widespread ownership of the smartphone means that nearly everyone has access to a camera at any given moment. However, some 4.5 million persons are seriously interested in photography as a hobby. They usually own more advanced cameras and additional photographic equipment such as extra lenses, tripods, electronic flash units, and filters. Often they have some interest in doing their own darkroom work.

With today's digital and automated cameras, fast films, and simplified processing methods, photography has become a rewarding hobby that offers many levels of satisfaction. As a visual activity it stimulates the photographer to see things in a new way. A successful photographer learns to see in a clear, sensitive, and perceptive manner.

Photography is an active hobby that can be enjoyed in connection with such interests and activities as nature study, gardening, or travel. Camera clubs can be found in many communities, schools, and colleges. Members often exchange information, share and discuss their work, and listen to guest lecturers. Workshops and short courses on photography are also available. And through blogs and social media, almost anyone can show their work to a wider community.

PHOTOGRAPHY AS A CAREER

Few vocations offer a greater variety of opportunities than does photography. Some professional photographers work as full-time employees, some run their own businesses, and some freelance.

Commercial photographers who work for advertising agencies photograph products for advertising promotions, brochures, catalogs, and other purposes. Their work can range from simple, straightforward shots to elaborate studio setups. Some commercial photographers may specialize in certain product areas, such as fashion, food, or hardware.

Portrait photographers take pictures of people, singly or in groups, for display in homes and offices. Wedding photographers take formal portraits of the bride, groom, and wedding party and also provide candid coverage of the ceremony.

Industry uses photographers to photograph plants, manufacturing processes, products, workers, and executives. Photographers who work on annual reports must produce pictures that are visually interesting and that show the corporation in a favourable light.

Photojournalism is a visual form of reporting. This 1966 Larry Burrows photo showed Americans back home what was happening on the front lines of the Vietnam War.

Photojournalists are reporters with cameras, photographing current events and people for newspapers, magazines, and the electronic media. This physically demanding, and sometimes dangerous, work requires both journalistic and photographic skills. Today most successful photojournalists are graduates of a journalism school that has a photojournalism department or offers photojournalism courses.

Many photographers enter the field professionally after gaining experience as amateurs. They may spend time as assistants or apprentices before striking out on their own.

Even after the advent of digital photography, there are a variety of opportunities for specialists and technicians in photography. For example, highly skilled darkroom technicians are still needed by custom labs that cater to professionals.

This resource focuses on the history of photography as a visual art. Beginning in 1839 with the invention and early evolution of the new medium, it takes a detour into the technology associated with photography, before examining its various genres. Finally, it examines the photographers of the 20th and 21st centuries and the works that advanced photography to its current accepted status of visual art.

CHAPTER ONE

THE INVENTION AND EARLY EVOLUTION OF PHOTOGRAPHY: c. 1839–1900

Photography is generally considered to have had its birth in 1839, when the Frenchman Louis-Jacques-Mandé Daguerre first revealed his photographic process to the public. The roots of photography, however, were developed much earlier.

ANTECEDENTS

The forerunner of the camera was the camera obscura, a dark chamber or room with a hole (later a lens) in one wall, through which images of objects outside the room were projected on the opposite wall. The principle was probably known to the Chinese and to ancient Greeks such as Aristotle more than 2,000 years ago. Late in the 16th century, the Italian

Children watching an outdoor scene through a camera obscura, 1887.

scientist and writer Giambattista della Porta demonstrated and described in detail the use of a camera obscura with a lens. While artists in subsequent centuries commonly used variations on the camera obscura to create images they could trace, the results from these devices depended on the artist's

CAMERA OBSCURA

The camera obscura is the ancestor of the photographic camera. The Latin name means "dark chamber," and the earliest versions, dating to antiquity, consisted of small darkened rooms with light admitted through a single tiny hole. The result was that an inverted image of the outside scene was cast on the opposite wall, which was usually whitened. For centuries the technique was used for viewing eclipses of the sun without endangering the eyes and, by the 16th century, as an aid to drawing; the subject was posed outside and the image reflected on a piece of drawing paper for the artist to trace. Portable versions were built, followed by smaller and even pocket models; the interior of the box was painted black and the image reflected by an angled mirror so that it could be viewed right side up. The introduction of a light-sensitive plate by Joseph-Nicéphore Niépce created photography.

drawing skills, and so scientists continued to search for a method to reproduce images completely mechanically.

In 1727 the German professor of anatomy Johann Heinrich Schulze proved that the darkening of silver salts, a phenomenon known since the 16th century and possibly earlier, was caused by light and not heat. He demonstrated the fact by using sunlight to record words on the salts, but he made no attempt to preserve the images permanently. His discovery, in combination with the camera obscura, provided the basic technology necessary for photography. It was not until the early 19th century, however, that photography actually came into being.

EARLY EXPERIMENTS

The medium that we know today is a result of generations of experimentation and development.

HELIOGRAPHY

Joseph-Nicéphore Niépce, an amateur inventor living near Chalon-sur-Saône, a city 189 miles (304 km) southeast of Paris, was interested in lithography, a process in which drawings are copied or drawn by hand onto lithographic stone and then printed in ink. Not artistically trained, Niépce devised a method by which light could draw the pictures he needed. He oiled an engraving to make it transparent and then placed it on a plate coated with a light-sensitive solution of bitumen of Judea (a type of asphalt) and lavender oil and exposed the setup to sunlight. After a few hours, the solution under the light areas of the engraving hardened, while that under the dark areas remained soft and could be washed away, leaving a permanent, accurate copy of the engraving. Calling the process heliography ("sun drawing"), Niépce succeeded from 1822 onward in copying oiled engravings onto lithographic stone, glass, and zinc and from 1826 onto pewter plates.

In 1826/27, using a camera obscura fitted with a pewter plate, Niépce produced the first successful photograph from nature, a view of the courtyard of his country estate, Gras, from an upper window of the house. The exposure time was about eight hours, during which the sun moved from east to west so that it appears to shine on both sides of the building.

Niépce produced his most successful copy of an engraving, a portrait of Cardinal d'Amboise, in 1826. It was exposed in about three hours, and in February 1827 he had the pewter plate etched to form a printing plate and had two prints pulled. Paper prints were the final aim of Niépce's heliographic process, yet all his other attempts, whether made by using a camera or by means of engravings, were underexposed and too weak to be etched. Nevertheless, Niépce's discoveries showed the path that others were to follow with more success.

THE DAGUERREOTYPE

Louis-Jacques-Mandé Daguerre was a professional scene painter for the theatre. Like many other artists of his time, Daguerre made preliminary sketches by tracing the images produced by both the camera obscura and the camera lucida, a prism-fitted instrument that was invented in 1807. His attempt to retain the duplication of nature he perceived in the camera obscura's ground glass led in 1829 to a partnership with Niépce, with whom he worked in person and by correspondence for the next four years. However, Daguerre's interest was in shortening the exposure time necessary to obtain an image of the real world, while Niépce remained interested in producing reproducible plates. It appears that by 1835, three years after Niépce's death, Daguerre had discovered that a latent image forms on a plate of iodized silver and that it can be "developed" and made visible by exposure to mercury vapour, which settles on the exposed parts of the image. Exposure times could thus be reduced from eight hours to 30 minutes. The results were not permanent, however; when the developed picture was exposed to light, the unexposed areas of silver darkened until the image was no longer visible. By 1837 Daguerre was able to fix the image permanently by using a solution of table salt to dissolve the unexposed silver iodide. That year he produced

Still Life, a daguerreotype by Louis Daguerre, 1837.

a photograph of his studio on a silvered copper plate, a photograph that was remarkable for its fidelity and detail. Also that year, Niépce's son Isidore signed an agreement with Daguerre affirming Daguerre as the inventor of a new process, "the daguerreotype."

LOUIS-JACQUES-MANDÉ DAGUERRE

Louis-Jacques-Mandé Daguerre was born on November 18, 1787, in Cormeilles, France. He was at first an inland revenue officer and then a scene painter for the opera. In 1822 at Paris he opened the Diorama, an exhibition of pictorial views, with various effects induced by changes in the lighting. A similar establishment that he opened in Regent's Park, London, was destroyed by fire in 1839.

Nicéphore Niépce, who since 1814 had been attempting to obtain permanent pictures by the action of sunlight, learned in 1826 of Daguerre's efforts in the same field. The two became partners in the development of Niépce's heliographic process from 1829 until the death of Niépce in 1833. Daguerre continued his experiments, and it was he who discovered that exposing an iodized silver plate in a camera would result in a lasting image if the latent image on the plate was developed by exposure to fumes of mercury and then fixed (made permanent) by a solution of common salt. On January 9, 1839, a full description of his daguerreotype process was announced at a meeting of the Academy of Sciences

by the eminent astronomer and physicist François Arago. Daguerre was appointed an officer of the Legion of Honour. In 1839 Daguerre and the heir of Niépce were assigned annuities of 6,000 francs and 4,000 francs, respectively, in return for their photographic process. Daguerre died on died July 10, 1851, in Bry-sur-Marne.

In 1839 Niépce's son and Daguerre sold full rights to the daguerreotype and the helio-graph to the French government, in return for annuities for life. On August 19 full working details were published. Daguerre wrote a book-let describing the process, *An Historical and Descriptive Account of the Various Processes of the Daguerreotype and the Diorama*, which at once became a best seller; 29 editions and translations appeared before the end of 1839.

PHOTOGENIC DRAWING

The antecedents of photogenic drawing can be traced back to 1802, when Thomas Wedgwood, son of the famous potter Josiah Wedgwood, reported his experiments in recording images on paper or leather sensitized with silver nitrate. He could record silhouettes of objects placed on the paper, but he was not able to make them permanent. Sir Humphry Davy published a paper in the *Journal of the Royal Institution*,

London, in June 1802, on the experiments of his friend Wedgwood; this was the first account of an attempt to produce photographs.

In 1833 the French-born photographer Hercules Florence worked with paper sensitized with silver salts to produce prints of drawings; he called this process "photography." However, since he conducted his experiments in Brazil, apart from the major scientific centres of the time, his contributions were lost to history until 1973, when they were rediscovered. Others in Europe, including one woman, claimed to have discovered similar photographic processes, but no verifiable proof has come to light.

William Henry Fox Talbot, trained as a scientist at the University of Cambridge, could not draw his scientific observations, even with the aid of a camera lucida; this deficiency inspired him to invent a photographic process. He decided to try to record by chemical means the images he observed, and by 1835 he had a workable technique. He made paper light-sensitive by soaking it alternately in solutions of common salt (sodium chloride) and silver nitrate. Silver chloride was thus produced in the fibres of the paper. Upon exposure to light, the silver chloride became finely divided silver, dark in tone. Theoretically, the resulting negative, in which tonal and spatial values were reversed, could be used to make any number of positives simply by putting fresh sensitized paper in contact with the negative and exposing it to light.

William Henry Fox Talbot.

Talbot's method of fixing the print by washing it in a strong solution of sodium chloride was inadequate, however, and the process was not successful until February 1839, when his astronomer friend Sir John Herschel suggested fixing the negatives with sodium hyposulphite (now called sodium thiosulfate) and waxing them before printing, which reduced the grain of the paper.

When news of Daguerre's process reached England in January 1839, Talbot rushed publication of his "photogenic drawing" process and

WILLIAM HENRY FOX TALBOT

William Henry Fox Talbot was born on February 11, 1800, in Melbury Sampford, Dorset, England. He was educated at Harrow and at Trinity College, Cambridge, and published many articles in the fields of mathematics, astronomy, and physics. He briefly served in Parliament (1833–34) and in 1835 published his first article documenting a photographic discovery, that of the paper negative. These so-called photogenic drawings were basically contact prints on light-sensitive paper, which unfortunately produced dark and spotty images.

In 1840 he modified and improved this process and called it the calotype (later the talbotype). Unlike the original process, it used a much shorter exposure time and a development process following exposure. Talbot patented the process in 1841 and was reluctant to share his knowledge with others, which lost him many friends and much information. In 1842 Talbot received a medal from the British Royal Society for his experiments with the calotype.

Talbot's *The Pencil of Nature* (1844–46), published in six installments, was the first book with photographic illustrations. Its 24 (of a proposed 50) plates document the beginnings of photography primarily through studies of art objects and architecture. In 1851 Talbot discovered a way of taking instantaneous photographs, and his "photolyphic engraving" (patented in 1852 and 1858), a method of using printable steel plates and muslin screens to achieve quality middle tones of photographs on printing plates, was the precursor to the development in the 1880s of the more successful halftone plates. Talbot died on September 17, 1877, near Chippenham, Wiltshire.

subsequently explained his technique in complete detail to the members of the Royal Society—six months before the French government divulged working directions for the daguerreotype.

THE REVOLUTION OF TECHNIQUE

Photography's remarkable ability to record a seemingly inexhaustible amount of detail was marveled at again and again. Still, from its beginnings, photography was compared—often unfavourably—with painting and drawing, largely because no other standards of picture making existed. Many were disappointed by the inability of the first processes to record colours and by the harshness of the tonal scale. Critics also pointed out that moving objects were not recorded or were rendered blurry and indistinct because of the great length of time required for an exposure.

Despite these deficiencies, many saw the technique of photography as a shortcut to art. No longer was it necessary to spend years in art school drawing from sculpture and from life, mastering the laws of linear perspective and chiaroscuro. Others saw these realizations as threatening. For example, upon first seeing the daguerreotype process demonstrated, the academic painter Paul

Delaroche declared, "From today, painting is dead"; although he would later realize that the invention could actually aid artists, Delaroche's initial reaction was indicative of that of many of his contemporaries. Such artists at first feared what Daguerre boasted in a 1838 broadsheet: "With this technique, without any knowledge of chemistry or physics, one will be able to make in a few minutes the most detailed views."

DEVELOPMENT OF THE DAGUERREOTYPE

Daguerre's process rapidly spread throughout the world. Before the end of 1839, travelers were buying daguerreotypes of famous monuments in Egypt, Israel, Greece, and Spain; engravings of these works were made and then published in two volumes as *Excursions daguerriennes* between 1841 and 1843. Although Daguerre's process was published "free to the world" by the French government, he took out a patent for it in England; the first licensee was Antoine-François-Jean Claudet. The first daguerreotypes in the United States were made on September 16, 1839, just four weeks after the announcement of the process. Exposures were at first of excessive length, sometimes up to an hour. At such lengthy exposures, moving objects could not be recorded, and portraiture was impractical.

Experiments were begun in Europe and the United States to improve the optical, chemical, and practical aspects of the daguerreotype process to make it more feasible for portraiture, the most desired application. The earliest known photography studio anywhere opened in New York City in March 1840, when Alexander Wolcott opened a "Daguerrean Parlor" for tiny portraits, using a camera with a mirror substituted for the lens. During this same period, József Petzval and Friedrich Voigtländer, both of Vienna, worked on better lens and camera design. Petzval produced an achromatic portrait lens that was about 20 times faster than the simple meniscus lens the Parisian opticians Charles Chevalier and N.M.P. Lerebours had made for Daguerre's cameras. Meanwhile, Voigtländer reduced Daguerre's clumsy wooden box to easily transportable proportions for the traveler. These valuable improvements were introduced by Voigtländer in January 1841. That same month another Viennese, Franz Kratochwila, freely published a chemical acceleration process in which the combined vapours of chlorine and bromine increased the sensitivity of the plate by five times.

The first studio in Europe was opened by Richard Beard in a glasshouse on the roof of the Royal Polytechnic Institution in London on March 23, 1841. Unlike the many daguerreotypists who were originally scientists or miniature painters, Beard had been a coal merchant and patent speculator. Having acquired the exclusive British license for the American mirror camera (he later also purchased the exclusive rights to Daguerre's invention in England, Wales, and the colonies), Beard employed the chemist John Frederick Goddard to try to improve and accelerate the exposure process. Among the techniques Goddard studied were two that Wolcott had tried: increasing the light sensitivity of the silver iodide with bromine vapours and filtering the blindingly bright daylight necessary for exposure through blue glass to ease the portrait sitter's eye strain. By December 1840 Goddard had succeeded well enough to produce tiny portraits ranging in size from 0.4 inch (1 cm) in diameter to 1.5 by 2.5 inches (4 by 6 cm). By the time Beard opened his studio, exposure times were said to vary between one and three minutes according to weather and time of day. His daguerreotype portraits became immensely popular, and the studio made considerable profits the first few years, but competition soon appeared, and Beard lost his fortune in several lawsuits against infringers of his licenses.

The finest daguerreotypes in Britain were produced by Claudet, who opened a studio on the roof of the Royal Adelaide Gallery in June 1841. He was responsible for numerous improvements in photography, including the discovery that red light did not affect sensitive plates and could therefore be used safely in the darkroom. The improvements that had been made in lenses and sensitizing techniques reduced exposure times to approximately 20 to 40 seconds.

Daguerreotyping became a flourishing industry. Practitioners such as Hermann Biow and Carl Ferdinand Stelzner worked in Germany, and William Horn opened a studio in Bohemia in 1841. It was the United States, however, that led the world in the production of daguerreotypes. Portraiture became the most popular genre in the United States, and within this genre, standards of presentation began to develop. Certain parts of the daguerreotype portrait, usually the lips, eyes, jewelry, and occasionally the clothing, were hand-coloured, a job often done by women. Because of their fragile nature, daguerreotype images always were covered with glass and encased in a frame or casing made of leather-covered wood or gutta-percha, a plasticlike substance made from rubber.

In the late 1840s every city in the United States had its own "daguerrean artist," and villages and towns were served by traveling photographers who had fitted up wagons as studios. In New York City alone there were 77 galleries in 1850. Of these, the most celebrated was that of Mathew B. Brady, who began in 1844 to form a "Gallery of Illustrious Americans," a collection of portraits of notables taken by his own and other cameramen. Several of these portraits, including those of Daniel Webster and Edgar Allan Poe, were published by lithography in a folio volume.

In Boston, Albert Sands Southworth and Josiah Johnson Hawes opened a studio in 1843 that was advertised as "The Artists' Daguerreotype Rooms"; here they produced the finest portraits ever made by the daguerreotype process. The partners avoided the stereotyped lighting and stiff posing formulas of the average daguerreotypist and did not hesitate to portray their sitters unprettified and "as they were." For example, in his portrait Lemuel Shaw, a judge of the Supreme Court of Massachusetts, stands with a crumpled coat and unruly locks of hair under a glare of sunshine; in her portrait Lola Montez—adventurer, dancer, actress—lolls over the back of a chair, a cigarette between her gloved fingers.

Cities and towns, as well as their inhabitants, were also photographed by American daguerreotypists: the rapid growth of San Francisco was documented month by month, and the first history of the city, published in 1855, was illustrated with engravings made from daguerreotypes.

Daguerreotyping spread throughout the world during the 1850s as photographers from England, France, and the United States followed colonialist troops and administrators to the Middle East, Asia, and South America. Army personnel and commercial photographers portrayed foreign dignitaries, landscape, archi-tecture, and monuments in order to show Westerners seemingly exotic cultures. Partic-ularly notable were daguerreotypes made in Japan by the American photographer Elipha-let Brown, Jr., who accompanied the 1853–54 mission led by Matthew C. Perry to open Japan to Western interests.

While most of the initial photographic work in these places was by Westerners, by the 1860s local practitioners had begun to open studios and commercial establishments. Marc Ferrez in Brazil, Kusakabe Kimbei in Japan, the (French-born) Bonfils family in Lebanon, and Kassian Céphas in Indonesia were among the inter-national photographers who set up studios to supply portraits and views during this period.

DEVELOPMENT OF THE CALOTYPE

The popularity of the daguerreotype sur-passed that of the photogenic drawing, but Talbot, convinced of the value of duplicability, continued to work to improve his process. On September 21–23, 1840, while experimenting with gallic acid, a chemical he was informed would increase the sensitivity of his prepared paper, Talbot discovered that the acid could be used to develop a latent image. This dis-covery revolutionized photography on paper as it had revolutionized photography on metal in 1835. Whereas previously Talbot had needed a camera exposure of one hour to produce a 6.5-by-8.5-inch (16.5-by-21.6-cm) negative, he now found that one minute was sufficient. Developing the latent image made photography on paper as valued as the daguerreotype, although the image still was not as clearly defined. Talbot named his improved negative process the calotype, from the Greek meaning "beautiful picture," and he protected his discoveries by patent.

The first aesthetically satisfying use made of this improved process was in the work of David Octavius Hill, a Scottish landscape painter, and his partner, Robert Adamson, an Edinburgh photographer. In 1843 Hill decided to paint a group portrait of the ministers who in that year formed

Hill and Adamson captured Scottish fishermen in this calotype from c. 1843.

the Free Church of Scotland; in all, there were more than 400 figures to be painted. Sir David Brewster, who knew of Talbot's process from the inventor himself, suggested to Hill that he make use of this new technique. Hill then enlisted the aid of Adamson, and together they made hundreds of photographs, not only of the members of the church meeting but also of people from all walks of life. Although their sitters were posed outdoors in glaring sunlight and had to endure exposures of upward of a minute, Hill and Adamson managed to retain a lifelike vitality. Hill's aesthetic was dominated by the painting style of the period in lighting and posing, particularly in the placement of the hands; in many of Hill's portraits, both the sitter's hands are visible, placed in a manner meant to add grace and liveliness to a dark portion of an image. Indeed, many of his calotypes are strikingly reminiscent of canvases by Sir Henry Raeburn and other contemporary artists. Proving the calotype's artistic qualities, William Etty, a royal academician, copied in oils the calotype Hill and Adamson made of him in 1844 and exhibited it as a self-portrait. In addition to their formal portraiture, the partners made a series of photographs of fishermen and their wives at Newhaven and in Edinburgh, as well as architectural studies.

The calotype, which lent itself to being manipulated by chemicals and paper, was used in the 1850s to create exceptionally artistic images of architectural monuments.

DAVID OCTAVIUS HILL

David Octavius Hill was born in Scotland in 1802. Originally a landscape painter, Hill made a name for himself at age 19 by publishing a series of lithographic landscapes. He was a founding member of the Royal Scottish Academy and was secretary of that organization for 40 years.

In 1843 he began to paint a large commemorative picture of the signing of the Deed of Demission, the act that marked the founding of the Free Church of Scotland. In order to get an accurate record of the features of the several hundred delegates to the founding convention, Hill decided to make photographic portraits and enlisted the collaboration of Robert Adamson, a young chemist who for a year had been experimenting with the calotype, a

(continued on the next page)

(continued from the previous page)

then-revolutionary photographic process that created the first "negative" from which multiple prints could be made. While Hill and Adamson made portraits of the delegates, most of the prominent Scots of the day came to watch the novel proceedings and have their own portraits made.

Hill preferred the calotype to the daguerreotype because it was less expensive. The calotype also suppressed details and allowed the photographer to control lighting, expression, and gesture and thereby to emphasize the sitter's personality. The portraits of George Meikle Kemp (before 1845), architect of the Sir Walter Scott Monument in Edinburgh, and of the sculptor John Henning (before 1849), show a masterful sense of form and composition and dramatic use of light and shade.

Between 1861 and 1862 Hill collaborated with Alexander McGlashan on a series of images made with collodion-glass negatives. He died on May 17, 1870, near Edinburgh, Scotland.

DEVELOPMENT OF STEREOSCOPIC PHOTOGRAPHY

Stereoscopic photographic views (stereographs) were immensely popular in the United States and Europe from about the mid-1850s

through the early years of the 20th century.
First described in 1832 by English physicist
Sir Charles Wheatstone, stereoscopy was
improved by Sir David Brewster in 1849. The production of the stereograph entailed making
two images of the same subject, usually with
a camera with two lenses placed 2.5 inches
(6 cm) apart to simulate the position of the
human eyes, and then mounting the positive
prints side by side laterally on a stiff backing.
Brewster devised a stereoscope through which
the finished stereograph could be viewed;
the stereoscope had two eye pieces through
which the laterally mounted images, placed
in a holder in front of the lenses, were viewed.
The two images were brought together by the
effort of the human brain to create an illusion
of three-dimensionality.

Stereographs were made of a wide range
of subjects, the most popular being views of
landscapes and monuments and composed
narrative scenes of a humorous or slightly
suggestive nature. Stereoscopes were manufactured for various price ranges and tastes,
from the simple hand-held device introduced
by Oliver Wendell Holmes (who promoted stereography through articles in *Atlantic Monthly*)
to elaborate floor models containing large
numbers of images that could be flipped
into place. The stereograph became especially popular after Queen Victoria expressed
interest in it when it was exhibited at the 1851

Crystal Palace Exposition. Like television today, stereography during the second half of the 19th century was both an educational and a recreational device with considerable impact on public knowledge and taste.

DEVELOPMENT OF THE WET COLLODION PROCESS

Photography was revolutionized in 1851 by the introduction of the wet collodion process for making glass negatives. This new technique, invented by the English sculptor Frederick Scott Archer, was 20 times faster than all previous methods and was, moreover, free from patent restrictions. Paper prints could easily be made from glass-plate negatives. The process had one major drawback: the photographer had to sensitize the plate almost immediately before exposure and expose it and process it while the coating was moist. Collodion is a solution of nitrocellulose (guncotton) in alcohol and ether; when the solvents evaporate, a clear plasticlike film is formed. Since it is then impervious to water, the chemicals used for developing the exposed silver halides and removing the unexposed salts cannot penetrate the coating to act upon them. The wet collodion process was almost at once universally adopted because it rendered detail with great precision that rivaled that of the daguerreotype. It reigned supreme for more than 30 years and greatly increased the popularity of photography, despite the fact that it was unequally sensitive to different colours of the spectrum.

FREDERICK SCOTT ARCHER

Frederick Scott Archer was born in 1813 in Bishop's Stortford, Hertfordshire, England. A butcher's son, Archer began his professional career as an apprentice silversmith in London, then turned to portrait sculpture. To assist him in this work, he began experimenting with the calotype photographic process of William Henry Fox Talbot.

In 1851 he described his wet collodion process, by which finely detailed glass negatives were produced; from these, paper positives could be printed. The plates had to be developed before the sensitized collodion dried after exposure, so that a darkroom tent and portable laboratory were needed for outdoor photography; but the new process produced such good results that it dominated photography for a generation. A

(continued on the next page)

(continued from the previous page)

lawsuit by Talbot claiming that the wet collodion was merely a variant of his own process was dismissed.

Archer also invented the ambrotype, a cheap form of portraiture, in collaboration with another photographer, but, having devoted all his funds to research, he died in poverty on May 2, 1857, in London.

At first the positive prints made from the glass plate negatives were produced by Talbot's salt paper method, but from the mid-1850s on they were made on albumen paper. Introduced in 1850 by Louis-Désiré Blanquart-Evrard, albumen paper is a slow printing-out paper (i.e., paper that produces a visible image on direct exposure, without chemical development) that had been coated with egg white before being sensitized. The egg white gave the paper a glossy surface that improved the definition of the image.

A new style of portrait utilizing albumen paper, introduced in Paris by André-Adolphe-Eugène Disdéri in 1854, was universally popular in the 1860s. It came to be called the *carte-de-visite* because the size of the mounted albumen print (4 by 2.5 inches [10.2 by 6 cm]) corresponded to that of a calling card. Disdéri used a four-lens camera to produce eight negatives on a single glass plate. Each picture could be separately posed, or several exposures of the same pose could be made at once. The principal advantage of the system was its economy: to make eight portraits the photographer needed to sensitize only a single sheet of glass and make one print, which was then cut up into separate pictures. At first *cartes-de-visite* almost invariably showed the subjects standing. Over time, backgrounds became ornate: furniture and such architectural fragments as papier-mâché columns and arches were introduced, and heavy-fringed velvet drapes were hung within range of the camera. With the advent of the cabinet-size (6.5 by 4 inches [16.5 by 10.2 cm]) picture in 1866, the decorative strategies of the photographer became yet more pronounced, so that in 1871 a photographer wrote: "One good, plain

This example of a *carte-de-visite* portrait was created sometime between 1860 and 1870.

background, disrobed of castles, piazzas, columns, curtains and what not, well worked, will suit every condition of life."

The new wet collodion process was also used to produce positive images on glass called ambrotypes, which were simply underexposed or bleached negatives that appeared positive when placed against a dark coating or backing. In pose and lighting, these popular portraits were similar to daguerreotypes in sizes and were enclosed in similar types of cases. They did not approach the brilliancy of the daguerreotype, however.

Tintypes, first known as ferrotypes or melainotypes, were cheap variations of the ambrotype. Instead of being placed on glass, the collodion emulsion was coated on thin iron sheets that were enameled black. At first they were presented in cases, surrounded by narrow gilt frames, but by the 1860s this elaborate presentation had been abandoned, and the metal sheets were simply inserted in paper envelopes, each with a cutout window the size of the image. Easy to make and inexpensive to purchase, tintypes were popular among soldiers in the Civil War and remained a form of folk art throughout the 19th century. Poses of sitters in tintypes were often informal and sometimes humorous. Because they were cheap and easy to produce, tintypes became a popular form of street photography well into the 20th century. Street-corner photographers, often equipped with a donkey, were common in European countries.

DEVELOPMENT OF THE DRY PLATE

In the 1870s many attempts were made to find a dry substitute for wet collodion so that plates could be prepared in advance and developed long after exposure, which would thereby eliminate the need for a portable darkroom. In 1871 Richard Leach Maddox, an English physician, suggested suspending silver bromide in a gelatin emulsion, an idea that led, in 1878, to the introduction of factory-produced dry plates coated with gelatin containing silver salts. This event marked the beginning of the modern era of photography.

Gelatin plates were about 60 times more sensitive than collodion plates. The increased speed freed the camera from the tripod, and a great variety of small hand-held cameras became available at relatively low cost, allowing photographers to take instantaneous snapshots. Of these, the most popular was the Kodak camera, introduced by George Eastman in 1888. Its simplicity greatly accelerated the growth of amateur photography, especially among women, to whom much of the Kodak advertising was addressed. In place of glass plates, the camera contained a roll of flexible negative material sufficient for taking 100 circular pictures, each roughly 2.5 inches (6 cm) in diameter. After the last negative was exposed, the entire camera was sent to one of the Eastman factories (Rochester, New York, or Harrow, Middlesex, England), where the roll was processed and printed; "You Press the Button, We Do the Rest" was Eastman's description of the Kodak system. At first Eastman's so-called "American film" was used in the camera; this film was paper based, and the gelatin layer containing the image was stripped away after development and fixing and transferred to a transparent support. In 1889 this was replaced by film on a transparent plastic base of nitro-cellulose that had been invented in 1887 by the Reverend Hannibal Goodwin of Newark, New Jersey.

GEORGE EASTMAN

George Eastman was born July 12, 1854, in Waterville, New York. After a public school education he worked briefly for an insurance company and a bank. In 1880 he perfected a process of making dry plates for photography and organized the Eastman Dry Plate and Film Company for their manufacture.

The first Kodak (a name he coined) camera was placed on the market in 1888. It was a simple handheld box camera containing a 100-exposure roll of film that used paper negatives. Consumers sent the entire camera back to the manufacturer for developing, printing, and reloading when the film was used up; the company's slogan was "You press the button, we do the rest."

In 1889 Eastman introduced roll film on a transparent base, which has remained the standard for film. In 1892 he reorganized the business as the Eastman Kodak Company. Eight years later he introduced the Brownie camera, which was intended for use by children and sold for one dollar. By 1927 Eastman Kodak had a virtual monopoly of the photographic industry in the United States, and it has continued to be one of the largest American companies in its field.

Eastman gave away half his fortune in 1924. His gifts, which totaled more than $75 million, went to such beneficiaries as the University of Rochester (of which the Eastman School of Music is a part) and the Massachusetts Institute of Technology. He was also one of the first business owners to introduce profit sharing as an employee

(continued on the next page)

(continued from the previous page)

incentive. On March 14, 1932, at the age of 77, Eastman took his own life, leaving a note that said, "My work is done. Why wait?" His home in Rochester, now known as George Eastman House, has become a renowned archive and museum of international photography as well as a popular tourist site.

PHOTOGRAPHY OF MOVEMENT

A few years before the introduction of the dry plate, the world was amazed by the photographs of horses taken by Eadweard Muybridge in California. To take these photographs, Muybridge used a series of 12 to 24 cameras arranged side by side opposite a reflecting screen. The shutters of the cameras were released by the breaking of their attached threads as the horse dashed by. Through this technique, Muybridge secured sets of sequential photographs of successive phases of the walk, the trot, and the gallop. When the pictures were published internationally in the popular and scientific press, they demonstrated that the positions of the animal's legs differed from those in traditional hand-drawn representations. To prove that his photographs were accurate, Muybridge projected them upon a screen one after the other with a lantern-slide projector he had built for the purpose; the result was the world's first motion-picture presentation. This memorable event took place at the San Francisco Art Association in 1880.

Muybridge, whose early studies were made with wet plates, continued his motion studies for some 20 years. With the new gelatin plates, he was able to improve his technique greatly, and in 1884–85, at the invitation of the University of Pennsylvania, he produced 781 sequential photographs of many kinds of animals as well as men and women engaged in a wide variety of activities. He was aided in this project by painter Thomas Eakins, who also made motion studies.

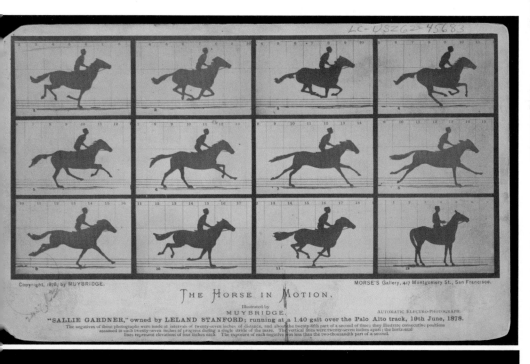

Eadweard Muybridge's 1878 photographs of a horse in motion contributed to the field of motion study.

Muybridge's photographic analysis of movement coincided with studies by French physiologist Étienne-Jules Marey to develop chronophotography. Whereas Muybridge had employed a battery of cameras to record detailed, separate images of successive stages of movement, Marey used only one, recording an entire sequence of movement on a single plate. With Marey's method, the images of various phases of motion sometimes overlapped, but it was easier to see and understand the flow of movement. Marey was also able to record higher speeds at shorter intervals than Muybridge. Both his and Muybridge's work greatly contributed to the field of motion study and to the development of the motion picture.

EARLY ATTEMPTS AT COLOUR

Photography's transmutation of nature's colours into various shades of black and white had been considered a drawback of the process from its inception. To remedy this, many portrait photographers employed artists who hand-tinted daguerreotypes and calotypes; artists also painted in oils over albumen portraits on canvas. Franz von Lenbach in Munich, for example, was among the many who projected onto canvas an image that had been made light-sensitive, whereupon he painted freely over it. In Japan, where hand-coloured woodcuts had a great tradition and labour was cheap, some firms from the 1870s onward sold photographs of scenic views and daily life that had been delicately hand-tinted. In the 1880s photochromes, colour prints made from hand-coloured photographs, became fashionable, and they remained popular until they were gradually replaced in the first decades of the 20th century by Autochrome plates.

CHAPTER TWO

ESTABLISHING GENRES

As the technology continued to develop, and as more and more people became involved in the medium, different and distinct types of photography emerged.

PORTRAITURE

From the medium's beginnings, the portrait became one of photography's most popular genres. Some early practitioners such as Southworth and Hawes and Hill and Adamson broke new ground through the artistry they achieved in their portraits. Outside such mastery, however, portraiture throughout the world generally took on the form of uninspired daguerreotypes, tintypes, *cartes-de-visite,* and ambrotypes, and most portraitists relied heavily on accessories and retouching. Such conventions were broken by several important subsequent photographers, notably Gaspard-Félix Tournachon, a Parisian writer, editor, and caricaturist who used the pseudonym of Nadar; Étienne Carjat, likewise a Parisian caricaturist; and Julia Margaret Cameron.

Nadar took up photography in 1853 as a means of making studies of the features of prominent Frenchmen for inclusion in a large caricature lithograph, the "Panthéon Nadar." He posed his sitters against plain backgrounds and bathed them with diffused daylight, which brought out every detail of their faces and dress. He knew most of them, and the powers of observation he had developed as a caricaturist led him to recognize their salient features, which he recorded directly, without the exaggeration that he put in his drawings. When Nadar's photographs were first exhibited, they won great praise in the *Gazette des Beaux Arts*, then the leading art magazine in France.

Gustave Eiffel, photographed by Nadar in 1888.

NADAR

The man who would be known as Nadar was born Gaspard-Félix Tournachon on April 5, 1820, in Paris. He began his career selling caricatures to humour magazines. By 1853, although he still considered himself primarily a caricaturist, Nadar had become an expert photographer and had opened a portrait studio. The space became a favourite meeting place of the intelligentsia of Paris. When in 1874 the painters later known as Impressionists needed a place to hold their first exhibit, Nadar lent them his gallery.

Nadar was a tireless innovator. In 1855 he patented the idea of using aerial photographs in mapmaking and surveying. It was not until 1858, however, that he was able to make a successful aerial photograph— the world's first—from a balloon. Nadar remained a passionate aeronaut until he and his wife and other passengers were injured in an accident in *Le Géant*, a gigantic balloon he had built.

In 1858 he began to photograph by electric light, making a series of photographs of Paris sewers. Later, in 1886, he made the first "photo interview," a series of 21 photographs of the French scientist

Michel-Eugène Chevreul in conversation. Each picture was captioned with Chevreul's responses to Nadar's questions, giving a vivid impression of the scientist's personality. Nadar also wrote novels, essays, satires, and autobiographical works until his death in Paris on March 21, 1910.

Carjat depicted the prominent Parisian artists, actors, writers, musicians, and politicians of his day. These portraits display dignity and distinction like those of Nadar, his contemporary and rival, but with a sometimes startling level of intensity in the sitters' gazes.

Cameron took up photography as a pastime in 1864. Using the wet-plate process, she made portraits of such celebrated Victorians of her acquaintance as Sir John F.W. Herschel, George Frederick Watts, Thomas Carlyle, Charles Darwin, and Alfred, Lord Tennyson. For her portraits, a number of which were shown at the Paris International Exhibition of 1867, Cameron used a lens with the extreme focal length of 30 inches (76.2 cm) to obtain large close-ups. This lens required such long exposures that the subjects frequently moved. The lack of optical definition and this accidental blurring was criticized by the photographic establishment, yet the power of her work won her praise among artists. This can be explained only by the intensity of her vision. "When I have had these men before

Julia Margaret Cameron captured this portrait of British naturalist and evolutionary theorist Charles Darwin circa 1870.

my camera," she wrote about her portraits of great figures,

> *my whole soul has endeavoured to do its duty toward them in recording faithfully the greatness of the inner man as well as the features of the outer man. The photograph thus obtained has almost been the embodiment of a prayer.*

Besides these memorable portraits, Cameron produced a large number of allegorical studies, as well as images of children and young women in costume, acting out biblical scenes or themes based on the poetry of her hero, Tennyson. In making these pictures—which some today find weak and sentimental—she was influenced by the

JULIA MARGARET CAMERON

Julia Margaret Pattle was born June 11, 1815, in Calcutta, India, the daughter of an officer in the East India Company. She married jurist Charles Hay Cameron in 1838. The couple had six children. After receiving a camera as a gift about 1863, she converted a chicken

(continued on the next page)

(continued from the previous page)

coop into a studio and a coal bin into a darkroom and began making portraits.

Among her sitters were her friends the poets Alfred, Lord Tennyson and Henry Wadsworth Longfellow, the astronomer Sir John Herschel, the writer Thomas Carlyle, and the scientist Charles Darwin. Especially noteworthy from this period are her sensitive renderings of female beauty.

Cameron was often criticized by the photographic establishment of her day for her supposedly poor technique: some of her pictures are out of focus, her plates are sometimes cracked, and her fingerprints are often visible. Later critics appreciated her valuing of spiritual depth over technical perfection and now consider her portraits to be among the finest expressions of the artistic possibilities of the medium.

In 1875 Cameron and her husband returned to their tea plantation in Ceylon, taking with them a cow, Cameron's photographic equipment, and two coffins, in case such items should not be available in the East. She continued to photograph and, according to legend, her dying word was "Beautiful!" She died on January 26, 1879.

Pre-Raphaelite painters, who portrayed similar themes in their work.

PHOTOJOURNALISM

From the outset, photography served the press. Within weeks after the French government's announcement of the process in 1839, magazines were publishing woodcuts or lithographs with the byline "from a daguerreotype." In fact, the two earliest illustrated weeklies—the *Illustrated London News*, which started in May 1842, and *L'Illustration*, based in Paris from its first issue in March 1843—owe their origin to the same cultural forces that made possible the invention of photography. Early reproductions generally carried little of the conviction of the original photograph, however.

Photography as an adjunct of war reportage began when Roger Fenton sailed from London to the Crimea to photograph the war between England, Russia, and Turkey in 1855. He was sent to provide visual evidence to counter the caustic written reports dispatched by William Russell, war correspondent for *The Times* of London, criticizing military mismanagement and the inadequate, unsanitary living conditions of the soldiers. Despite the difficulties of developing wet-collodion plates with impure water, in high temperatures, and under enemy fire, during his four-month stay Fenton produced 360 photographs, the first large-scale camera documentation of a war. Crimean War imagery was also captured by British photographer James Robertson, who later traveled to India with an

ROGER FENTON

Born in Heywood, England, in 1819, Roger Fenton studied painting and then law. Following a trip in 1851 to Paris, where he probably visited with the photographer Gustave Le Gray, he returned to England and was inspired to pursue photography. In the winter of 1855 his governmental connections as the founder and first honorary secretary of the Royal Photographic Society helped him gain an appointment as official photographer of the Crimean War.

Fenton and his assistant, Marcus Sparling, arrived on the ship *Hecla* and set up their darkroom in a wagon. Using the wet-collodion photographic process of the times, they took approximately 360 photographs of the war. As an agent of the government, however, Fenton portrayed only the "acceptable" parts of the conflict. Even the disastrous charge of the **Light Brigade was depicted as glorious. Although little of the real action or agony of war was shown, the images were nevertheless the first to depict the more mundane aspects of modern warfare.**

Upon Fenton's return to England, his war images were successfully exhibited in London and Paris, and wood engravings of the particularly notable photographs were printed in the *Illustrated London News*. Fenton continued to photograph architecture and landscapes until 1862, when he retired from photography and returned to practicing law. He died on August 8, 1869, in London.

associate, Felice Beato, to record the aftermath of the Indian Mutiny of 1857–58.

When the Civil War broke out in the United States, Mathew B. Brady, a New York City daguerreotypist and portraitist, conceived the bold plan of making a photographic record of the hostilities. When told the government could not finance such an undertaking, he invested his own savings in the project, expecting to recover his outlay by selling thousands of prints. Brady and his crew of about 20 photographers— among them Alexander Gardner and Timothy H. O'Sullivan, who both left his employ in the midst of hostilities—produced an amazing record of the battlefield. At his New York gallery, Brady showed pictures of the dead at Antietam. The *New York Times* reported on October 20, 1862:

Grand review of the Union army in Washington, D.C., May 1865, photograph by Mathew B. Brady.

Mr. Brady has done something to bring home to us the terrible reality and earnestness of war. If he has not brought bodies and laid them on our dooryards and along the streets, he has done something very like it. . . . It seems somewhat singular that the same sun that looked down on the faces of the slain blistering them, blotting out from the bodies all semblance to humanity, and hastening corruption, should have thus caught their features upon canvas, and given them per-petuity for ever. But it is so.

MATHEW BRADY

Born circa 1823 near Lake George, New York, Mathew B. Brady opened his first daguerreotype studio in New York City in 1844. His studio was highly publicized, and in 1845 he began to carry out his plan to photograph as many famous people of his time as he could—including Daniel Web-ster, Edgar Allan Poe, and James Fenimore Cooper. Brady had an extensive personal collection of presidential portraits: except for William Henry Harrison, who died only a month after his inauguration, Brady cre-ated, copied, or collected the photographs

(continued on the next page)

(continued from the previous page)

of every U.S. president from John Quincy Adams to William McKinley.

At the outbreak of the American Civil War in 1861, Brady decided to make a complete record of that conflict. He hired a staff of about 20 photographers and dispatched them throughout the war zones. Brady's main activities in the endeavour involved organizing and supervising the operation of his employees and studios; he himself probably photographed only occasionally on such battlefields as Bull Run, Antietam, and Gettysburg.

The Civil War project ruined Brady financially. He had invested $100,000 in it and had bought supplies on credit, confident that the government would buy his photographs after the war ended. The government, however, showed no interest. The financial panic of 1873 forced him to sell his New York studio and declare bankruptcy. He was unable to pay the storage bill for his negatives, which the War Department finally bought at public auction for $2,840. Through the efforts of his friends in government, Brady was finally granted $25,000 by Congress in 1875, but he never regained financial solvency. He died alone and virtually forgotten in a New York City hospital charity ward on January 15, 1896.

Throughout the remainder of the 19th century, intermittent conflicts in Asia and Africa arising from imperialist ambitions were documented by photographers working for news media and for companies that manufactured stereographs. For the most part, war images were accepted as truthful depictions of painful events. However, after images of the Communard uprising in Paris in 1871 were shown to have been doctored, the veracity of such camera documentation no longer could be taken for granted.

Regular use of photographs in magazines began with the perfection of the halftone process, which allowed the camera image to be printed at the same time as the type and thereby reduced the cost of reproduction. The first newspaper halftone in the United States appeared in 1888, and shortly thereafter newspapers turned to photography for reporting topical events, making the profession of newspaper illustrator obsolete. Although technical advances improved reproduction quality, apart from impressive examples of combat photography, the subjects and styles of early journalistic photography were generally unimaginative and dull.

DOCUMENTARY PHOTOGRAPHY

From the earliest days of the medium, landscape, architecture, and monuments were appealing subjects for photographers. In addition, the recognition of the power of photography to persuade and inform led to a form of documentary photography known as social documentation, or social photography.

LANDSCAPE AND ARCHITECTURAL DOCUMENTATION

This sort of photography, which was collected by artists, scientists, and travelers, was impelled by several factors. In Europe one powerful factor was the maneuverings among western European powers for control of portions of North Africa and Asia. From the late 1850s through the 1870s, British photographers were particularly active in recording the natural landscape and monuments of the empire's domains: Francis Frith worked in Egypt and Asia Minor, producing three albums of well-composed images; Samuel Bourne photographed throughout India (with a retinue of equipment bearers); John Thomson produced a descriptive record of life and landscape in China; and French photographer Maxime Du Camp traveled to Egypt with Gustave Flaubert on a government commission to record landscape and monuments.

Both for patriotic reasons and as a commodity for travelers, photographers also were active in recording the landscape of western Europe in the 1850s and '60s. Important British

MAXIME DU CAMP

An outgoing, adventurous man, Maxime Du Camp (born February 8, 1822, in Paris) also pioneered in photography and published works in virtually every literary genre. He traveled widely with the novelist Gustave Flaubert (1844–45 and 1849–51), and his *Égypte, Nubie, Palestine et Syrie* (1852), written after one of their journeys, is among the first books illustrated with photographs. During the revolutionary year 1848 he was wounded and then decorated for counter-revolutionary activity in France. His *Expédition des deux-Siciles* (1861; "Expedition to the Two Sicilies") recounted his experiences as a volunteer with the Italian revolutionary Giuseppe Garibaldi.

In 1851 Du Camp founded the *Revue de Paris* and in it published Flaubert's great novel, *Madame Bovary*; disputes arising from the publication of the novel ended their friendship. To *La Revue des Deux Mondes*, Du Camp contributed his *Paris, ses organes, ses fonctions et sa vie*, 6 vol. (1869–75; "Paris, Its Mechanisms, Its Workings, and Its Life"), an extensive document of the city. He also wrote poems (*Les Chants modernes*, 1855; "Modern Songs"), art criticism,

(continued on the next page)

(continued from the previous page)

novels, a monograph on his friend, the writer Théophile Gautier, and *Souvenirs littéraires*, 2 vol. (1882–83; "Literary Recollections"), which included previously unrevealed information about Flaubert and his struggles with epilepsy. Du Camp died on February 9, 1894, in Baden-Baden, Germany.

photographers included Roger Fenton, who worked in England and Wales; Charles Clifford, who worked in Spain; Robert Macpherson, who photographed Rome; and George Washington Wilson, who photographed Scotland. French photographer Adolphe Braun recorded the landscape around his native Alsace, as well as the mountainous terrain of the French Savoy, as did the brothers Louis-Auguste and Auguste-Rosalie Bisson. Herman Krone in Germany and Giacchino Altobelli and Carlo Ponti in Italy were also intent on recording the beauties of their regional landscapes.

Photographs of specific historical buildings were made for a number of purposes: to satisfy antiquarian curiosity, to provide information for restoration, to supply artists with material on which to base paintings, or to effect preservation efforts. Practically from photography's inception, such documentation was commissioned by public and private authorities. In western Europe and the United States, photographs captured the building of the industrial infrastructure, from bridges to railroad lines, from opera houses to public places to monumental statuary. In the early 1850s Philip Henry Delamotte was hired to document the progress of the construction of the Crystal Place in London, and a few years later Robert Howlett depicted the building of the Great Eastern transatlantic steamship. Alfred and John Bool and Henry Dixon worked for the Society for Photographing Old London, recording historical buildings and relics. In the 1850s the French government commissioned several photographers to document historical buildings. Working with cameras making photographs as large as 20 by 29 inches (51 by 74 cm), Henri Le Secq, Charles Marville, and Charles Nègre produced remarkable calotypes of the cathedrals of Notre-Dame (Paris), Chartres, and Amiens, as well as other structures that were being restored after centuries of neglect. An establishment was set up in Lille, France, by Blanquart-Evrard at which these paper negatives could be printed in bulk.

In the United States explorations of the lands beyond the Great Plains led to the apogee of landscape photography during the period. Before the Civil War, relatively few exceptional images of the Western landscape had been made. In the postwar era railroad

WAR DEPARTMENT, CORPS  OF ENGINEERS, U.S. ARMY.

Geographical Explorations and Surveys West of the 100ᵗʰ Meridian   Expedition of 1873 Under Command of Lieut. Geo.M.Wheeler,Corps of En⸗rs.

T.H.O'Sullivan, Phot.   N° 11

ANCIENT RUINS IN THE CAÑON DE CHELLE, N.M.

In a niche 50 feet above present Cañon bed.

American photographer Timothy O'Sullivan captured many Civil War scenes as an apprentice to Mathew B. Brady before turning to landscape photography, as shown here.

companies and government commissions included photographers among their teams sent to determine mineral deposits, rights of way, and other conditions that would be suitable for settlement. Of the photographers confronting the spectacular landscape of the American West in the 1870s and '80s, William Henry Jackson, O'Sullivan, and Carleton Watkins produced particularly notable work. Both O'Sullivan, who helped survey Nevada and New Mexico, and Watkins, who worked in California and Oregon, were able to convey through their work a sense of the untamed and extraordinary quality of the Western landscape. As a testament to the power of his images, Jackson's photographs of the Grand Canyon and the Yellowstone River were influential in getting public land set aside for Yellowstone National Park. The work these and other photographers of the American West produced usually was made available in several sizes and formats, from stereographic images to mammoth-sized works.

Landscapes in places outside the United States and Europe were usually portrayed by European photographers during this period. However, exceptions included the Chinese photographer Afong Lai and the Brazilian photographer Marc Ferrez, both of whom produced excellent views of their native countries. In particular, Lai's serene compositions reflected the conventions of

CARLETON WATKINS

Carleton E. Watkins was born November 11, 1829, in Oneonta, New York. At age 22, Watkins moved to California, and by the early 1860s, his reputation as a field photographer was firmly established. Watkins's images were large and clear, and he seemed able almost always to select the spot which, in his words, "would give the best view." His association with members of the California intellectual and artistic elite helped transform him from a competent craftsman into a photographer of great artistry.

His first significant landscape project involved making large-format images of Yosemite Valley. These photographs were influential in President Lincoln's decision to name Yosemite a national preserve. Because of these photographs, Mount Watkins in Yosemite was named in his honour.

Watkins also traveled extensively. He photographed the Columbia River region and Mount Shasta, parts of southern California and Arizona, Nevada's Comstock mines, and Yellowstone National Park. His work was exhibited extensively and won medals in expositions throughout the United States

and Europe. Following the loss of his entire studio in the 1906 San Francisco earthquake and fire, Watkins became ill and destitute, and in 1910 he was committed to a hospital for the insane. He died on June 23, 1916, in Imola, California.

the long-standing tradition of Chinese land-scape painting.

SOCIAL DOCUMENTATION

The origins of the genre can be traced to the classic sociological study issued by Henry Mayhew in 1851, *London Labour and the London Poor*, although this was illustrated with drawings partly copied from daguerre-otypes by Richard Beard and not actual photos. A later effort, *Street Life in London* (1877), by Adolphe Smith and John Thomson, included facsimile reproductions of Thom-son's photographs and produced a much more persuasive picture of life among Lon-don's working class. Thomson's images were reproduced by Woodburytype, a process that resulted in exact, permanent prints but was costly because it required hand mount-ing for each individual print. This pursuit was continued by John Barnardo, who, begin-ning in the 1870s, photographed homeless children in London for the purpose of both record keeping and fund-raising and thus fulfilled the double objectives of social documentation: capturing theoretically objective description and arousing sympathy. The "before" and "after" images used by Barnardo to demonstrate the efficacy of social intervention became a convention in social documentation. It was taken up to good effect by the Indian photographer Raja Lala Deen Dayal, especially in his documentation of the good works undertaken by the nizam of Hyderabad in the late 19th century. In 1877 Thomas Annan began a project in Edinburgh in which he used the camera to record the need for new housing for the working poor. He concentrated mainly on the derelict buildings and sewerage systems rather than on the inhabitants; eventually the images were collected for their artistic merit rather than their social use.

Social documentation became more focused in the work of Jacob A. Riis, a police reporter in New York City in the 1880s who spent about four years depicting slum life. Employing cameramen at first, Riis eventually learned the rudiments of the medium so that he could himself portray the living and working conditions of immigrants whose social circumstances, he believed, led to crime and dissolution. Reproduced by the recently developed halftone process, the photographs and drawings based on them illustrated *How the Other Half Lives* (1890), Riis's first book about immigrant life. They also were turned into positive transparencies—slides—to illustrate Riis's lectures, which were aimed at a largely middle-class audience, some of whom were said to have fainted at the sight of the conditions the images documented. Able to convince the progressive reformers of the time of the need

Baby in a Slum Tenement (1888–89), by Jacob Riis, was a part of a large-scale documentory project of the living conditions of the poor in New York City.

for change, Riis's work was instrumental in effecting slum-clearance projects in New York.

In European countries especially, there was also an awakened interest in documenting social customs during this period. Sometimes this meant recording those European customs that were being replaced by advancing industrialization. This interest led to the establishment of photographic

JACOB A. RIIS

Jacob August Riis was born on May 3, 1849, in Ribe, Denmark. He immigrated to the United States at the age of 21 and held various jobs, gaining a firsthand acquaintance with the ragged underside of city life. In 1873 he became a police reporter, assigned to New York City's Lower East Side, where he found that in some tenements the infant death rate was one in 10. Riis employed the newly invented flashbulb technique in photographing the rooms and hallways of these buildings in order to dramatize his lectures and books.

His book of documentary photography, *How the Other Half Lives* made him famous. The response of the future U.S. president Theodore Roosevelt was: "I have read your book, and I have come to help." The book stimulated the first significant New York legislation to curb tenement house evils. The illustrations were largely line drawings based on Riis's photographs. A reprint in 1971 included 30 photographs on which the original illustrations were based and 70 related Riis photographs. Of Riis's many other books, the most noteworthy was his autobiography, *The Making of an American* (1901). He died May 26, 1914, in Barre, Massachusetts.

archives, such as the National Photographic Record Association, set up in the mid-1890s by Benjamin Stone, a British member of Parliament. Left to the city of Birmingham, the collection included photographs taken by Stone and others of vanishing local customs. Other times this led to an interest in the particularities of dress and custom of those living in distant regions. William Carrick, a Scotsman, portrayed daily life in Russia. In addition to portraying nature and artifacts, John Thomson, Felice Beato, and Samuel Bourne also depicted indigenous peoples in China and India. In 1888 the journal *National*

Geographic, which produced photographic accounts of cultures throughout the world, was established.

PHOTOGRAPHY AS ART

Photographic societies—made up of both professionals and amateurs enticed by the popularity of the collodion process—began to form in the mid-19th century, giving rise to the consideration of photography as an aesthetic medium.

EARLY DEVELOPMENTS

In 1853 the Photographic Society, parent of the present Royal Photographic Society, was formed in London, and in the following year the Société Française de Photographie was founded in Paris. Toward the end of the 19th century, similar societies appeared in German-speaking countries, eastern Europe, and India. Some were designed to promote photography generally, while others emphasized only artistic expression. Along with these organizations, journals promoting photography as art also appeared.

At the first meeting of the Photographic Society, the president, Sir Charles Eastlake (who was then also president of the Royal Academy), invited the miniature painter Sir

William Newton to read the paper "Upon Photography in an Artistic View" (*Journal of the Photographic Society*, 1853). Newton's argument was that photographs could be useful so long as they were taken "in accordance [as far as it is possible] with the acknowledged principles of Fine Art." One way the photographer could make his results more like works of art, Newton suggested, was to throw the subject slightly out of focus. He also recommended liberal retouching. (Eastlake's wife, Lady Eastlake, née Elizabeth Rigby, was one of the first to write lucidly about the artistic problems of collodion/albumen photography.)

In response to this desire to create photographs that would fit an established conception of what "art" should be, several photographers began to combine several negatives to make one print. These consisted of compositions that were considered too complicated to be photographed in a straightforward manner and thus pushed photography beyond its so-called mechanical capabilities. A famous example of this style was by O. G. Rejlander, a Swede who had studied art in Rome and was practicing photography in England. He joined 30 negatives to produce a 31-by-16-inch (79-by-41-cm) print entitled *The Two Ways of Life* (1857), an allegory showing the way of the blessed led through good works and the way of the damned through vice. Rejlander, who described the technique in detail in photographic journals, stated that his purpose was to prove to artists the aesthetic possibilities of photography, which they had generally denied. The photograph was shown in the Manchester Art Treasures Exhibition of 1857 and was purchased by Queen Victoria for Prince Albert.

Rejlander's technique stimulated Henry Peach Robinson, a professional photographer who had been trained as an artist, to produce similar combination prints. He achieved fame with a five-negative print,

O. G. REJLANDER

Oscar Gustav Rejlander was born in 1813 in Sweden. He studied painting and sculpture in Rome before settling in England to practice photography. Rejlander rejected contemporary conceptions of photography as a scientific or technical medium. In his efforts to elevate photography to the status of a fine art, he made photographs in imitation of painting. He looked to the example of the Old Masters for their use of composition and pose and often set up his own elaborate compositions in his studio. In many of his works he sought painterly effects by combining several negatives to make one print, with a resulting image that moved beyond the results achieved by straightforward photography.

His most famous work, *The Two Ways of Life* (1857), was based on the background and arrangement of Raphael's *School of Athens* (1509–11) and was created by combining more than 30 negatives. Shown in the Manchester Art Treasures Exhibition of 1857, the photograph was purchased by Queen Victoria as a gift for Prince Albert. Rejlander was also well known for his ability to capture an emotion or sentiment in his work. A series of photographs of facial expressions and gestures made by Rejlander was used by Charles Darwin in his *Expression of the Emotions in Man and Animals* (1872).

Although he had a period of critical acclaim, Rejlander died impoverished in 1875. His influence extended for decades, however, as photographers began to debate the merits of Pictorialism, or the effort to achieve painterly effects, versus the value of more sharply detailed work.

Fading Away, produced in 1858. The subject, a dying girl, was considered by critics as too painful a subject to be represented by photography. Perhaps the implied authenticity of the camera bothered them, since painters had long presented subjects of a far more sensitive nature.

Fading Away is an 1858 print by Henry Peach Robinson. The combination print shows a young girl on her deathbed surrounded by family.

Robinson became an articulate member of the Photographic Society, and his teaching was even more influential than his photography. In 1869 the first of many

HENRY PEACH ROBINSON

Henry Peach Robinson was born July 9, 1830, in Ludlow, Shropshire, England. At age 21 he was an amateur painter precocious enough to have one of his paintings hung at the Royal Academy in London. Photography, however, was his real passion. In 1857 he opened a photographic studio in Leamington, England. In addition to commercial portraiture, he began to make photographs that imitated the themes and compositions of the anecdotal genre paintings popular at the time. He created photographs such as *Juliet with the Poison Bottle* (1857), his earliest-known work, by combining separate negatives into a composite picture, utilizing a process known as combination printing. Although he sometimes used natural settings, he more often imitated the out-of-doors inside his studio.

(continued on the next page)

(continued from the previous page)

Costumed actors or society ladies modeled for his many bucolic scenes, since he found actual country people too awkward and dull to fit his ideal of the picturesque.

In 1858 Robinson exhibited *Fading Away*, a picture skillfully printed from five different negatives. This work depicted the peaceful death of a young girl surrounded by her grieving family. Although the photograph was the product of Robinson's imagination, many viewers felt that such a scene was too painful to be tastefully rendered by such a literal medium as photography. The controversy, however, made him the most famous photographer in England and the leader of the Pictorialist movement, which advocated achieving painterly effects in photography.

Robinson's subsequent works, such as *The Lady of Shalott* (1861) and *Autumn* (1863), were so widely admired that he published *Pictorial Effect in Photography* (1869), a handbook that for decades remained the most influential work in English on photographic practice and aesthetics. This work and essays by Robinson based on it were widely printed and translated, giving his aesthetic ideas great currency. In 1886, however, the book was violently attacked by the photographer

Peter Henry Emerson, who argued that photographic images should never be altered after exposure and also decried Robinson's practice of using costumed models and painted backdrops. Nevertheless, Robinson continued to receive official honours, and in 1892 he became a founding member of the Linked Ring, an association of prestigious art photographers. He died February 21, 1901, in Tunbridge Wells, Kent.

editions and translations of his book, *Pictorial Effect in Photography*, was published. Robinson borrowed compositional formulas from a handbook on painting, claiming that use of them would bring artistic success. He stressed the importance of balance and the opposition of light against dark. At the core of his argument was the assumption that rules set up for one art form could be applied to another.

So long as photographers maintained that the way to photography as art was the emulation of painting, art critics were reluctant to admit the new medium to an independent aesthetic position. Portraits, when done as sensitively and as directly as those produced by Hill and Adamson, Nadar, and Cameron, won praise. But sentimental genre scenes, posed and arranged for the camera and lacking the truthfulness thought to be characteristic of photography, were the subject of considerable controversy. This debate would reach a crescendo at the end of the century.

NATURALISTIC PHOTOGRAPHY

Opposing the strategies advocated by Robinson, in the 1880s the English physician and photographer Peter Henry Emerson proposed that photographs should reflect nature, offer "the illusion of truth," and be produced without using retouching techniques, recombining multiple prints, or utilizing staged settings, models, and costumes. He believed that the unique qualities of tone, texture, and light inherent in photography made it a unique art form, making any embellishments used for the sake of "art" unnecessary. This is not to say his own photographs were purely documentary—in fact, his work in some ways mimicked the artistic effects of the Barbizon school and Impressionist painting—but they eschewed the manipulated artistic effects of his contemporaries. Emerson's views, known as naturalistic photography, gained a considerable audience through his widely read 1889 publication entitled *Naturalistic Photography* and through numerous articles that appeared in photography journals throughout the 1890s.

PICTORIALISM AND THE LINKED RING

The ideas of Newton, Rejlander, Robinson, and Emerson—while seemingly varied—all pursued

PETER HENRY EMERSON

Born May 13, 1856, in Cuba, Peter Henry Emerson was trained as a physician. He first began to photograph as a part of an anthropological study of the peasants and fishermen of East Anglia. He soon became convinced that photography was a medium of artistic expression superior to all other black-and-white graphic media because it reproduces the light, tones, and textures of nature with unrivaled fidelity. He was repelled by the contemporary fashion for composite photographs, which imitated sentimental genre paintings. In his hand-book *Naturalistic Photography* (1889), he decreed that a photograph should be direct and simple and show real people in their own environment, not costumed models posed before fake backdrops or other such predetermined formulas.

(continued on the next page)

(continued from the previous page)

Emerson's book was very persuasive, but in 1891 he published a black-bordered pamphlet "The Death of Naturalistic Photography," in which he recanted his opinion that the accurate reproduction of nature was synonymous with art. Despite his change of mind, his initial views remained influential and formed the rationale of much 20th-century photography. Emerson died May 12, 1936, in Falmouth, Cornwall, England.

the same goal: to gain acceptance for photography as a legitimate art form. These efforts to gain acceptance were all encompassed within Pictorialism, a movement that had been afoot for some time and that crystallized in the 1890s and early 1900s, when it was promoted through a series of international exhibiting groups. In 1892 the Brotherhood of the Linked Ring was founded in Britain by Robinson, George Davison, a leader of the Art Nouveau movement, and others dissatisfied with the scientific bias of the London Photographic Society. The group held annual exhibitions, which they called salons. While the members' work varied from naturalism to staged scenes to manipulated prints, by the turn of the century it was their united belief that "through the *Salon* the Linked Ring has clearly demonstrated that pictorial photography is able to stand alone

Peter Henry Emerson's *A Rusty Shore* (1886) captures the natural simplicity of an English reed bed.

and that it has a future entirely apart from that which is purely mechanical." Similar Pictorialist groups formed in other countries. These included the Photo-Club of Paris, the Trifolium of Austria, and like associations in Germany and Italy. Unity of purpose enabled members to exchange ideas and images with those who had similar outlooks in other countries.

CHAPTER THREE

PERFECTING THE MEDIUM: 1900–1945

As the new century dawned, a new generation of photographers emerged who were determined to turn away from the Pictorial style and its soft-focus, painterly effects to a more direct, unmanipulated, and sharply focused approach. This new form was called "straight" photography, and its practitioners believed it most truly expressed photography's unique vision.

THE PHOTO-SECESSION

At the turn of the 20th century, one of the most influential Pictorialist groups was the Photo-Secession, founded in New York City in 1902 by photographer Alfred Stieglitz. The Secession's name was taken from the avant-garde secessionist movements in Europe that sought to differentiate themselves from what they considered outmoded ways of working and thinking about the arts. With the help of Edward Steichen, Stieglitz opened the Little Galleries of the Photo-Secession—popularly known as "291" after its address on Fifth Avenue—which exhibited the work of Modernist painters and sculptors as well as that of photographers who used a wide variety of printing processes, including gum-bichromate and bromoil printing. These procedures required considerable handwork and resulted in one-of-a-kind prints that in their softening effects resembled etchings or lithographs rather than photographs. Among the members of the Photo-Secession were Steichen, Alvin Langdon Coburn, Gertrude Käsebier, and Clarence H. White. Between 1903 and 1917 Stieglitz published 50 issues of the beautifully printed journal *Camera Work*, which contained, among other works, fine gravure reproductions of American and European photographs and halftone reproductions of artwork by Henri Matisse and Pablo Picasso.

ALFRED STIEGLITZ

The first photographer to have his work exhibited in American art museums, Alfred Stieglitz (1864–1946) was also a devoted supporter of Modern art, particularly Modern

(continued on the next page)

(continued from the previous page)

American art. The Photo-Secession group he founded in 1902 contributed to the acceptance of photography as an art form. The group's gallery, which opened in 1905, was officially named the Little Galleries of the Photo-Secession, but because it was located at 291 Fifth Avenue in New York City, it soon came to be referred to as 291. Stieglitz used the gallery to provide a showcase for many European and American artists, including August Rodin, Henri Matisse, Paul Cézanne, Pablo Picasso, Georgia O'Keeffe, John Marin, and Arthur Dove.

Stieglitz was born in Hoboken, New Jersey, on January 1, 1864. He went to school in New York City until 1881, when the family moved to Europe. After studying mechanical engineering at the Berlin Polytechnic in Germany for a few months in 1883, Stieglitz became interested in photography and decided to study photochemistry instead. He was responsible for notable technical innovations that allowed the taking of photographs in rain, in snow, and at night.

Stieglitz moved to the United States in 1890. Frustrated by public unwillingness to accept photography as an art form, he assembled a group of talented American photographers and founded the Photo-Secession. He was also largely responsible for the public recognition of contemporary American artists. One of the artists whose work was seen for the first time at 291 was Georgia O'Keeffe. She and Stieglitz were married in 1924. In addition to his other work, Stieglitz edited and published *Camera Work*. This magazine appeared between 1903 and 1917 and included beautifully reproduced photographs as well as articles that advanced the cause of serious photography.

After 291 closed in 1917, Stieglitz devoted more time to photography. In New York City and at his summer home in Lake George, New York, he created a famous series of photographic portraits of O'Keeffe and also a group of photographs of cloud patterns, whose abstract shapes suggest various emotions. Between 1925 and 1929 he opened two other galleries in New York City.

Stieglitz's prints were the first photographs to be received as works of art by major museums in Boston; New York City; and Washington, D.C. He died on July 13, 1946, in New York City.

Over the 15-year period of the Photo-Secession's existence, the outlook of Stieglitz and individual members changed, reflecting the general move away from the more artificial aspects of Pictorialism as the 20th century began. Increasingly, photographers wanted their work to look like photographs, not paintings, and valued the qualities that were unique to photography. Over time, 291 began to show more painting than photography, and, as Stieglitz became even more convinced of the value of "straight," rather than manipulated, photographic printing, several original adherents fell away, among them Käsebier and White. The final two issues of *Camera Work* were devoted to "straight" work by Paul Strand, who was the only photographer Stieglitz considered promising at the time. Strand's images, consisting mainly of New York views and close-up portraits (made with a 45-degree prism lens so that the subject was unaware of being photographed), combined pure formal qualities, such as beautiful tone and sharp focus, with intense feeling.

Blind Woman, New York, photograph by Paul Strand, 1916.

THE NEW OBJECTIVITY

In the period immediately following World War I, much photography was characterized by sharply defined imagery, especially of objects removed from their actual context. The clean lines and cool effects of this style—variously called the "New Objectivity," the "new vision," or "Precisionism"—was a reflection, perhaps, of the overarching role of industry and technology during the 1920s.

Strand, continuing in the direction he had unveiled in 1917, produced powerful, highly detailed close-ups of machines and organic matter and made sparkling landscapes in Gaspé, Quebec, and the American West. His approach changed again when he was invited to Mexico to produce educational films for the government. There he made a series of portraits (again with the prism lens) and landscapes, which he published in 1940 as gravure prints. Steichen, who had been in command of aerial photography for the American Expeditionary Forces, abandoned his earlier impressionistic handling in favour of crisp, sharply focused celebrity, fashion, and product images, which appeared in *Vanity Fair* and *Vogue* magazines. Others whose sharp, well-designed images of industrial products appeared in advertising brochures and magazines included Margaret Bourke-White, Paul Outerbridge, and Charles Sheeler.

MARGARET BOURKE-WHITE

Margaret Bourke-White was born on June 14, 1904, in New York City. Throughout the 1930s Bourke-White went on assignments to create photo-essays in Germany, the Soviet Union, and the Dust Bowl in the American Midwest. These experiences introduced people and social issues as subject matter into her oeuvre, and she developed a compassionate, humanitarian approach to such photos. In 1935 Bourke-White met the Southern novelist Erskine Caldwell, to whom she was married from 1939 to 1942. The couple collaborated on three illustrated books.

Bourke-White became one of the first four staff photographers for *Life* magazine when it began publication in 1936. She covered World War II for *Life* and was the first woman photographer attached to the U.S. armed forces. While crossing the Atlantic to North Africa her transport ship was torpedoed and sunk, but Bourke-White survived to cover the bitter daily struggle of the Allied infantrymen in the Italian campaign. She then covered the siege of Moscow and, toward the end of the war, she crossed the Rhine River into Germany with General George Patton's Third Army troops. Her photographs of the emaciated inmates of concentration camps and of the corpses in gas chambers stunned the world.

After World War II, Bourke-White traveled to India to photograph Mahatma Gandhi and record the mass migration caused by the division of the Indian subcontinent into Hindu India and Muslim Pakistan. During the Korean War she worked as a war correspondent and traveled with South Korean troops.

Stricken with Parkinson disease in 1952, Bourke-White continued to photograph and write. She retired from *Life* magazine in 1969 and died August 27, 1971, in Connecticut.

A preference for a straight, highly detailed presentation of natural and manufactured forms also characterized the work of California photographer Edward Weston. Using large-format (8-by-10-inch [20.3-by-25.4-cm]) equipment with lenses stopped down to the smallest aperture, Weston, whose earlier career had been in commercial portraiture, formulated a method of "rendering the very substance and quintessence of the thing itself, whether it be polished steel or palpitating flesh." Further, Weston, like Strand, did not approve of cropping or handwork of any kind on the negative; both held that the final image should be composed in the ground glass of the camera prior to exposure.

Several Californians, a number of whom looked to Weston as a mentor, took up the concentration on organic forms and objects and the preference for using the smallest aperture of the lens to create maximum depth of field and sharpness. Known as Group f.64, for the smallest lens aperture, the group included, besides Weston and his son Brett, Ansel Adams and Imogen Cunningham. After

Dunes, Oceano, photograph by Edward Weston, 1936.

seeing Strand's negatives, Adams decided to pursue photography as a profession, specializing in photographing Western wilderness areas such as Yosemite National Park and the Sierra Nevada mountain range. His dramatic photographs masterfully captured the beauty of such natural wonders, and the popularity of his photographs helped raise awareness of the importance of preservation efforts. He also was a teacher of great persuasiveness who advocated the exact control of tonal quality through what he called the "zone system."

In Europe this approach of favouring extremely sharp definition was known as Neue Sachlichkeit ("New Objectivity"). Its outstanding proponents were the German photographers Karl Blossfeldt and Albert Renger-Patzsch. Blossfeldt made highly detailed and magnified images of plants, removed from their natural habitat. Renger-Patzsch, a professional photographer in Essen, was fascinated by the formal qualities of everyday objects, both organic and manufactured. Like those of his American counterparts, his images featured strong design components and stressed the materiality of substances rather than the maker's emotional attitude toward the subject. He too believed that the final image should exist in all its completeness before the exposure was made and that it should be an unmanipulated record. Renger-Patzsch's ideas and images, published in 1928 in *Die Welt ist schön* ("The World Is Beautiful") and translated into a number of languages, exerted considerable influence on European photography of the time. Hans Finsler, of Swiss origin and working in Germany, Piet Zwart in the Netherlands, and Emmanuel Sougez and Florence Henri in France were among the many producing highly defined close-ups of objects and people in a style similar to that of the Neue Sachlichkeit.

A similarly objective approach characterized the work of photographers interested in the artistic ideas embodied in Constructivism; the movement proposed that photographs could be a means to present the commonplace from fresh vantage points and thereby reawaken interest in routine objects and processes. This idea, which originated in the Soviet Union and spread quickly to Germany and central European countries during the late 1920s and early 1930s, granted greater latitude for experimentation with form. Its foremost spokesman was Russian painter and ideologue Aleksandr Rodchenko, who employed distinctly unusual vantage points in order to give the mundane world a new appearance. The visual ideas underpinning Constructivism appealed to Hungarian photographer László Moholy-Nagy, who reinterpreted them during his tenure first at the Bauhaus in Weimar, then in

Dessau, Germany, and later at the School of Design in Chicago, where they influenced several generations of American photographers.

Similar ideas were utilized by photographers in Japan, especially following the earthquake of 1923. Among those whose imagery reflected the new sharper style, with its emphasis on form rather than atmosphere, was Yasuzō Nojima, who gained a reputation for his incisive portraits, groundbreaking nudes, and landscapes. Shinzō Fukuhara's photographs, particularly his landscapes, were also highly regarded.

EXPERIMENTAL APPROACHES

By 1916 abstract ideas were appealing to a number of other photographers. Photo-Secessionist Alvin Langdon Coburn, living in England, created a series of photographs known as vortographs, in which no subject matter is recognizable. During the late 1910s, students and faculty at the Clarence H. White School of Photography (started by another former colleague of Stieglitz), in particular Bernard S. Horne and Margaret Watkins, also produced works that displayed the influence of Modernist abstraction.

Between the two world wars, an experimental climate—promoted by Constructivist ideology and by Moholy-Nagy and the Bauhaus—

admitted an entire range of new directions in photography. One aspect of this experimentalism involved eschewing subject matter and instead creating photographs that more closely resembled abstract paintings. Photographers again manipulated images, experimented with processes, and used multiple images or exposures. Sometimes, rather than experimenting with the camera itself, they experimented with light and sensitized paper. For a brief time this direction was allied with Dadaist ideas about accident, chance, and the subconscious. One important exponent of photographic experimentalism was the American expatriate Dada artist Man Ray, whose "rayographs," photographs that appeared

MAN RAY

Man Ray was born Emmanuel Radnitzky on August 27, 1890, in Philadelphia, Pennsylvania. The son of a tailor and seamstress, he grew up in New York City, where he studied architecture, engineering, and art, and became a painter. As a young man, he was a regular visitor to Alfred Stieglitz's 291 gallery, where he was exposed to current art trends and earned an early appreciation for photography. In 1915 Man Ray met the French artist Marcel Duchamp, and together they collaborated on many inventions and formed the New York group of Dada artists. Like Duchamp, Man Ray began to produce ready-mades, commercially manufactured objects that he designated as works of art. Among his best-known ready-mades is *The Gift*, a flatiron with a row of tacks glued to the bottom.

Man Ray moved to Paris and became associated with the Parisian Dada and Surrealist circles of artists and writers. His experiments with photography included rediscovering how to make "cameraless" pictures, made by placing objects directly on light-sensitive paper, which he exposed to light and developed.

Man Ray also pursued fashion and por-trait photography. Many of his photographs were published in magazines such as *Harper's Bazaar*, *Vu*, and *Vogue*. He continued his experiments with photography through the genre of portraiture. Man Ray also made films. In one short film, he applied the rayo-graph technique to motion-picture film, making patterns with salt, pepper, tacks, and pins.

(continued on the next page)

(continued from the previous page)

In 1940 Man Ray escaped the German occupation of Paris by moving to Los Angeles. Returning to Paris in 1946, he continued to paint and experiment until his death. His autobiography, *Self-Portrait*, was published in 1963. He died November 18, 1976, in Paris.

as series of swirling abstract shapes, were created without a camera by exposing objects placed on sensitized paper to light.

Cameraless photography, which came to be called "light graphics," also appealed to Moholy-Nagy and his wife, Lucia Moholy, who called the products of their experimentation "photograms." Photographs made by using this kind of manipulation of light could have completely abstract shapes or forms or feature recognizable objects. A number of artists in central Europe also manipulated light and objects to produce abstract images; among them were Jaroslav Rössler and Gyorgy Kepes, who eventually taught at the Chicago Institute of Design. There Kepes was instrumental in introducing its methods to American photographers, among them Carlotta Corpron, who produced a series of abstractions by using a device, called a light modulator, favoured at the Bauhaus.

The manipulative strategies of photocollage and montage had considerable appeal during the interwar period in part because—by appropriating "content" from other sources—

they could deal with complex political or psychological feelings and ideas. Czech and German artists were especially drawn to this type of experimentation. Herbert Bayer, Raoul Hausmann, John Heartfield, and Hannah Höch were unusually adept in their innovative use of collage and montage to make ironic comments on a range of political and social issues in German society. Heartfield, whose work appeared on book jackets and posters, savaged the political thuggery behind the rise of Nazism by juxtaposing political imagery—for example, a stock photograph of Hitler—with unexpected, provocative imagery. Höch concentrated on portraying the role of the "new woman" emerging in the chaos of postwar German society; for example, the title of one work by Höch, *Cut with the Kitchen Knife*, suggests a female domain, yet the image shows women freed from housewifely duties, cavorting among machinery and political figures as part of the world at large. Similarly, montage enabled Soviet Constructivists to suggest complex ideas, as in El Lissitzky's self-portrait, which integrates drafting tools and geometric shapes to suggest that the artist himself was an architect of society.

DOCUMENTARY PHOTOGRAPHY

Working mainly in the opening years of the 20th century, French photographer Eugène

Atget documented shop fronts, architectural details and statuary, trees and greenery, and individuals who made their living as street vendors, producing some 10,000 photographs of Paris and its environs. Unlike many of the architectural photographers before him, Atget showed a remarkable attention to composition, the materiality of substances, the quality of light, and especially the photographer's feelings about the subject matter. His work was bought mainly by architects, painters, and archivists. The visually expressive force of Atget's work, produced with a large-format camera, is a testament to the capacity of documentation to surpass mere record making to become inspiring experience.

In like manner, although not as extensively, Czech photographer Josef Sudek created an artistic document of his immediate surroundings. He was particularly fascinated with his home and garden, often shooting the latter through a window.

Lewis W. Hine created a similarly thorough document of a subject, in his case immigrant and working-class life in the United States. One of the first to refer to himself as a social photographer, Hine began his documentation of immigrants at Ellis Island while still a teacher at the Ethical Culture School in New York. Eventually he gave up teaching to work for the National Child Labor Committee, an organization of progressives seeking to make

Men's Fashions, photograph by Eugène Atget, 1925.

the American industrial economy more aware of its effects on individual workers. From 1908 to 1916 Hine concentrated on photographing child workers, producing thousands of individual portraits and group scenes of underage children employed in textile mills, mines, canning establishments, and glass factories and in street trades throughout the United States. His work was effective in prompting first state regulation and eventually federal regulation of child labour.

Documentary photography experienced a resurgence in the United States during the Great Depression, when the federal government undertook a major documentary project. Produced by the Farm Security Administration (FSA) under the direction of Roy E. Stryker, who earlier had come in contact with Hine's work, the project comprised more than 270,000 images produced by 11 photographers working for varying lengths and at different times in different places. All worked to show the effects of agricultural displacement caused by the economic downturn, lack of rain, and wasteful agricultural practices in the American South and midlands. In this project, documentation did double duty. One task was to record conditions both on nonfunctioning farms and in new homesteads created by federal legislation. Another was to arouse compassion so that problems addressed by legislative action would win support. A portrait of a migratory

Migrant Mother, Nipomo, California by Dorothea Lange.

pea picker's wife, made by California portrait-ist turned documentarian Dorothea Lange, became an icon of the anxiety generated by the Great Depression.

DOROTHEA LANGE

Born on May 26, 1895, in Hoboken, New Jersey, Lange studied photography at Columbia University. In 1918 she traveled around the world, earning money as she went by selling her photographs. Her money ran out by the time she got to San Francisco, so she settled there and obtained a job in a photography studio.

During the Great Depression, Lange began to photograph the unemployed men who wandered the streets of San Francisco. Pictures such as *White Angel Breadline* (1932), showing the desperate condition of these men, were publicly exhibited and received immediate recognition both from the public and from other photographers. These photographs also led to a commission in 1935 from the Farm Security Administration [FSA], which hoped that Lange's powerful images would bring the conditions

of the rural poor to the public's attention. FSA director Roy Styker considered her most famous portrait, *Migrant Mother, Nipomo, California*, to be the iconic representation of the agency's agenda. The work now hangs in the Library of Congress.

In 1941 she received a Guggenheim Fellowship, and the following year she recorded the mass evacuation of Japanese-Americans to detention camps after Japan's attack on Pearl Harbor. After World War II she created a number of photo-essays, including *Mormon Villages* and *The Irish Countryman*, for *Life* magazine. Lange died October 11, 1965, in San Francisco, California. The next year she was honoured with a retrospective show at the Museum of Modern Art in New York City.

Walker Evans was another photographer whose work for the FSA transformed social documentation from mere record making into transcendent visual expression. On leave from the FSA, Evans worked with James Agee on *Let Us Now Praise Famous Men* (1941; reissued 1966), a compelling look at the lives of a family of Southern sharecroppers. Although unaffiliated with the FSA, Margaret Bourke-White, formerly one of the era's foremost industrial photographers, also worked in the South. With her husband, writer Erskine Caldwell, she produced *You Have Seen*

Their Faces (1937), one of the first photographic picture books to appear in softcover.

Documentary projects underwritten by other federal agencies also existed. One of the more significant projects was executed by Berenice Abbott. Inspired in part by Atget's studies of Paris, she endeavoured to photograph the many parts of New York City and to create "an intuition of past, present, and future." She was able to interest the Works Progress Administration (WPA) in underwriting an exhibit and publication along these lines entitled *Changing New York* (1939). Other urban documentary projects were undertaken under the aegis of the Photo League, an association of photographers of varying background and class who set out to document working-class neighbourhoods in New York.

The German portraitist August Sander, intent on creating a sociological document of his own, generated a portrait of Germany during this period. His focus was on the individuals composing German society, documenting a class structure with workers and farmers on the bottom. Sander's inclusion of types not considered Aryan by German authorities brought him into conflict with the Nazi regime, which destroyed the plates for a proposed book entitled *Antlitz der Zeit* ("Face of Our Time").

Among the many other amateur and professional photographers who interested themselves in the documentation of everyday life were Sergey Prokudin-Gorsky, who portrayed everyday life in Russia; Manuel Alvarez Bravo, who created images that offer a psychologically nuanced glimpse of Mexican life; and Robert Doisneau and Brassaï, both of whom captured vibrant images of everyday life in Paris. Perhaps the most extensive ethnographic documentation was that of Edward S. Curtis, who produced 20 volumes of studies of Native American tribespeople over the course of

Sergey Prokudin-Gorsky portrayed everyday life in Russia in saturated colour.

some 20 years. The enormous interest in how people outside Western culture appeared and behaved was a factor in the increasing popularity of *National Geographic* during this period.

PHOTOJOURNALISM

Toward the end of the 19th and into the early 20th century, greater numbers of magazines were published throughout the world. The enlarged demand for photographic illustration, along with the appearance of lighter, easier-to-use camera equipment, led to an increase in images of war for reproduction. The Spanish-American War was documented by Jimmy Hare, the South African War by Horace W. Nicholls, the Russo-Japanese War by Luigi Barzini, and the Mexican Revolution by Augustin Victor Casasola. Although strict censorship prevailed with regard to the photographic record of World War I, the prominence of picture magazines from the 1920s through the 1950s ensured the continuance of war reportage.

A new approach to photojournalism began to emerge with the appearance of the Ermanox in 1924 and the Leica in 1925. These two German-made miniature cameras, fitted with wide-aperture lenses, required extremely short exposure times for outdoor work and were even able to photograph indoor scenes with available light. The Leica had the added advantage of using 35-mm roll film that could be advanced quickly, allowing a succession of exposures to be made of the same subject. This capability led to photographs whose informality of pose and sense of presence were remarkable.

Owing to these developments, the photojournalist was able to perceive a significant moment in a fraction of a second and to use the camera with such speed and precision that the instantaneous perception would be preserved forever. This is evident in the work of the Hungarian André Kertész in Paris during the 1920s. The Frenchman Henri Cartier-Bresson began about 1930 to develop the style that he later called

Henri Cartier-Bresson's photographs helped establish photojournalism as an art form.

the search for the "decisive moment." To him the camera was an "extension of the eye." Preferring the miniature 35-mm-film camera, he worked unobtrusively, making numerous exposures that usually included one in which all the elements come together to form a compelling psychological and visual statement.

In 1928–29 two of the largest picture magazines in Europe, the *Münchner Illustrierte Presse* and the *Berliner Illustrirte Zeitung*, began to print the new style of photographs. Erich Salomon captured revealing candid portraits of politicians and other personalities by sneaking his camera

HENRI CARTIER-BRESSON

With his Leica camera, French photographer Henri Cartier-Bresson (1908–2004) traveled the world, recording the images he saw. His humane, spontaneous photographs helped establish photojournalism as an art form.

Cartier-Bresson was born in Chanteloup, near Paris, on August 22, 1908. In the late 1920s he studied painting both in Paris and at Cambridge University in England. But exhibits of the photographs of Man Ray and Eugène Atget, two major 20th-century photographers, triggered his fascination with the camera.

In 1931 he traveled to Africa with a miniature camera. He bought his first Leica 35-millimeter camera in 1933. His first journalistic photography was created in Spain during that country's civil war in the late 1930s. There he produced his first documentary film—on medical aid in the war. This experience stimulated an interest in motion pictures, and he worked as an assistant to the film director Jean Renoir.

During World War II Cartier-Bresson was imprisoned by the Germans, but he escaped in 1943 and joined the French underground. In 1947 he helped found, along with Robert Capa, the freelance agency Magnum Photos. There were many exhibits of his work, including a 1955 traveling exhibition, before his photographs were put in the National Library in Paris. In later years most of Cartier-Bresson's interest was in motion pictures. He died on August 3, 2004, in Céreste, France.

into places and meetings officially closed to photographers. Felix H. Man, encouraged by Stefan Lorant, editor of the *Münchner Illustrierte*, made sequences of photographs at interviews and cultural and social events, which Lorant then laid out in imaginative picture essays.

The example of the German picture magazines was followed in other parts of Europe and in the United States. One was the short-lived *Vu*, established in Paris in 1928. An issue of *Vu* devoted entirely to the Spanish Civil War contained memorable photographs by Robert Capa. In 1936 both *Life* and *Look* were conceived in the United States, and a formula evolved in which the picture editor, photographer, researcher, and writer constituted a team.

Among *Life*'s first photographers were Bourke-White, already famous for her industrial photographs made largely for the magazine *Fortune*; Alfred Eisenstaedt, an experienced photo reporter for the Keystone Picture Agency in Germany; Hansel Mieth, also from Germany, who at times worked with her husband, Otto Hagel; and Peter Stackpole, whose photographs of the Golden Gate Bridge in San Francisco attracted much attention. The concept of *Life* from the start, according to its founder, Henry Luce, was to replace haphazard picture taking and editing with the "mind-guided camera." Photographers were briefed for their assignments and encouraged to take great quantities of photographs so that the editors might have a large selection. (The fact that selection and sequencing were a function of the editors led to objections on the part of some photographers, notably W. Eugene Smith, who left the employ of *Life* at one point in order to gain greater control over his own work.) The visual organization of the picture story was carefully planned for maximum reader impact.

The opening photograph of the photo-essay established the situation, and as with written narration there was a visual climax and a definite conclusion.

Initially *Life* and *Look* preferred to use pictures of great sharpness and depth. Thus, instead of unobtrusive miniature cameras, American photographers used large-format cameras requiring slow lenses, large plates, and additional flash light. This way of photographing was challenged by Lorant, who had left the *Münchner Illustrierte Presse* after being forced to leave Germany in 1934. He eventually settled in London, where he established the magazines *Weekly Illustrated* (1934) and *Picture Post* (1938). Staff photographers on both magazines included old colleagues also forced from Germany, such as Man and Kurt Hutton. They and other contributors were encouraged to develop the technique and pictorial style of taking photographs by using available light—i.e., not using a flash. Their pictures had a remarkable naturalness that brought great reader appeal—so much so that *Life* began to publish similar photographs and in 1945 hired a former *Picture Post* photographer, Leonard McCombe, with an extraordinary clause in his contract: he was forbidden to use a flash.

The photojournalistic style popularized by *Life* and *Look* influenced other activity in the field, in particular the exhibition "Family of Man," which was mounted by Steichen at the Museum of Modern Art in New York City in 1955. This highly popular exhibition presented over 500 photographs—mostly photojournalistic and documentary work—alongside texts of different sizes and formats, somewhat in the manner of a three-dimensional magazine.

Memorable groups of photographs were taken for the major picture magazines. Examples are *Man's A Day with Mussolini*, first published in the *Münchner Illustrierte Presse* (1931) and then, with a brilliant new layout, in *Picture Post*; Smith's *Spanish Village* (1951) and *Nurse Midwife* (1951) in *Life*; and Eisenstaedt's informal, penetrating portraits of famous Britons, also in *Life*. Images by Eisenstaedt of the Italian incursion into Ethiopia and by David Seymour ("Chim") and Capa of the Spanish Civil War made visible events leading up to World War II. This conflict was thoroughly documented for the Western allies by military personnel as well as by Capa, Bourke-White, Dmitry Baltermants, Yevgeny Khaldey, and Constance Stuart Larrabee on the North African, eastern European, and western European fronts and by Smith in the South Pacific. Heinrich Hoffman portrayed the war at home and at the front for Germany, and Yosuke Yamahata documented the role of the Japanese army in the South Pacific.

Eugene Smith captured this photograph of U.S. soldiers saluting the flag during World War II for *Life* magazine.

COLOUR PHOTOGRAPHY

The Autochrome process, introduced in France in 1907 by Auguste and Louis Lumière, was the first practical colour photography process. It used a colour screen (a glass plate covered with grains of starch dyed to act as primary-colour filters and black dust that blocked all unfiltered light) coated with a thin film of panchromatic (i.e., sensitive to all colours) emulsion, and it resulted in a positive colour transparency. Because Autochrome was a colour transparency and could be viewed only by reflected light, however, researchers continued to look for improvements and alternative colour processes.

In 1935 Leopold Godowsky, Jr., and Leopold Mannes, two American musicians working with the Kodak Research Laboratories, initiated the modern era of colour photography with their invention of Kodachrome film. With this reversal (slide) film, colour transparencies could be obtained that were suitable both for projection and for reproduction. A year later the Agfa Company of Germany developed the Agfacolor negative-positive process, but owing to World War II the film did not become available until 1949. Meanwhile, in 1942 Kodak introduced the Kodacolor negative-positive film that 20 years later—after many improvements in quality and speed and a great reduction in price—would become the most popular film used for amateur photography.

THE DEVELOPMENT OF KODACHROME

Leopold Mannes and Leopold Godowsky, Jr., school friends who enjoyed a mutual interest in music and photography, set up a small laboratory for experimentation with colour film. In 1919 the two created a mediocre colour film, at which time they realized that the additive process they had been working with would not give them the true colours that they sought. It was at this point that Mannes and Godowsky switched to a multiple-layered subtractive-film approach that would eventually lead them to the development of Kodachrome.

They opened their first real laboratory in New York City in 1922, and with the backing of Dr. C. E. Kenneth Mees of the Eastman Kodak Company in 1930, the duo moved to Rochester, New York, to work with assistants at the well-equipped Kodak Research Laboratories. On April 15, 1935, Kodachrome's development was announced as the earliest of the colour-subtractive films that proved a boon to colour photography. Though originally used for animated motion pictures, Kodachrome was later improved and used widely until 2009, when it was discontinued.

NOTABLE PHOTOGRAPHERS OF THE ERA

There are countless photographers from this time who were instrumental in advancing the medium of photography. Following are brief biographical sketches of just a sampling.

PAUL STRAND

Combining realism and abstraction in photographs of landscapes and close-ups of rocks and plants, Paul Strand (1890–1976) achieved a synthesis in a style he described as organic realism. He was also one of the first photographers to use the candid-camera technique.

Strand was born on October 16, 1890, in New York City. At age 17 he enrolled in classes taught by Lewis Hine, a pioneer in photojournalism. Hine took his students to the 291 Gallery, run by Alfred Stieglitz. Abstract forms and patterns in the Cubist paintings on display there greatly influenced Strand. In 1916 he was given his first one-man show at 291.

After serving in World War I, Strand traveled to Colorado, Maine, Quebec, and New Mexico and photographed landscapes to capture what he described as "the spirit of the place." He also worked as a freelance motion-picture cameraman. In 1932 Strand was appointed chief of photography and cinematography by the Mexican government. He later formed Frontier Films to make documentaries. Strand settled in France in 1950. He died near Paris on March 31, 1976.

CHARLES SHEELER

Born on July 16, 1883, in Philadelphia, Charles Sheeler studied at the School of Industrial Art in Philadelphia and then at the Pennsylvania Academy of Fine Arts.

To make a living, Sheeler turned to photography. Initially he worked on assignments from Philadelphia architects. He moved to New York City in 1919 and the next year collaborated with the photographer Paul Strand on a film, *Mannahatta*, a study of the buildings of the city. During the early 1920s he received recognition for both his paintings and his photography. In 1927 he made an outstanding series of photographs of the Ford Motor Company's plant at River Rouge, Michigan.

In 1929 he painted one of his best-known pictures, *Upper Deck*, which has been acclaimed for its pristine, geometric surfaces. *Rolling Power*, another major work, emphasized the abstract power of the driving wheels of a locomotive. Sheeler also treated architectural subjects in his abstract-realist style. His later works tended toward a less literal rendering of their subjects. Sheeler died on May 7, 1965, in Dobbs Ferry, New York.

EDWARD WESTON

An artist obsessed with realism, the American photographer Edward Weston (1886–1958) refused to manipulate his images in the darkroom. One of the most influential photographers of the 20th century, he preferred to work in abstract forms found in nature with high-resolution detail in his photographs.

Weston was born in Highland Park, Illinois, on March 24, 1886. He began his professional career as a portrait photographer in Glendale, California His early work was in the style he later rejected—that of the Pictorialists, photographers who imitated the soft-focus images of impressionistic paintings.

In 1923 he moved to Mexico. Back in California in 1927, he made monumental close-ups of seashells and vegetables. His photographs of rocks and trees on Point Lobos, California, were published in *The Art of Edward Weston* (1932). A series of nudes and sand dunes begun in 1936 is often considered his finest work. In 1937, aided by a Guggenheim fellowship, he started taking the photographs that appeared in *California and the West* (1940). Stricken by Parkinson's disease shortly afterward, Weston began taking his last Point Lobos pictures. They appeared in *My Camera on Point Lobos* (1950). He died in Carmel, California, on January 1, 1958.

ANSEL ADAMS

The American photographer Ansel Adams (1902–84) was well known for technical innovations and for his dramatic pictures of Western landscapes. He was a pioneer in the movement to preserve the wilderness and one of the first to promote photography as an art form.

Ansel Adams was born in San Francisco, California, on February 20, 1902. Originally a student of music, he took photographs only as a hobby until 1927. In that year he published his first portfolio, *Parmellian Prints of the High Sierras*. ("Parmellian" refers to the texture of mountain surfaces.) The style was Pictorialist, similar to that of impressionist painting with its soft, misty images rather than detailed likenesses.

In 1930 Adams adopted the straight photography style of the United States photographer Paul Strand, whose photographs emphasized tones and sharp detail. Two years later, with another photographer, Adams formed Group f.64, an association of photographers who used large cameras and small apertures (lens openings) to capture an infinite variety of light and texture. Contact prints were rich in detail and brilliant in showing tonal differences; subjects were portrayed in the most vivid way. Adams soon became one of the outstanding technicians in the history of photography. In 1935 he published *Making a Photograph*, the first of many books that he produced on photographic technique.

In 1941 Adams began making photomurals for the United States Department of the Interior. Their large scale forced him to master techniques for photographing the light and space of immense landscapes. He developed what he called the zone system, a method of determining beforehand, for each part of the scene, what the final tone would be.

Throughout his career Adams worked to increase public acceptance of photography as a fine art. He felt that an artist's final product was really no different from an artistically created photograph, intended to be preserved and respected. In 1940 he helped found the world's first museum collection of photographs at the Museum of Modern Art in New York City. In 1946 he established, at the California School of Fine Arts in San Francisco, the first academic department to teach photography as a profession.

From the time of his adolescence, Adams had a serious interest in preserving the environment. From 1936 he was a director of the Sierra Club, a group founded in 1892 to preserve the scenic beauty of particular areas in the United States. Many of Adams' books are pleas for the preservation of nature: *My Camera in the National Parks* (1950), *This Is the American Earth* (1960), and *Photographs of the Southwest* (1976). Adams also published some general photographic anthologies, including Ansel Adams: Images, 1923–1974 (1974) and *The Portfolios of Ansel Adams* (1977).

IMOGEN CUNNINGHAM

Born on April 12, 1883, in Portland, Oregon, Imogen Cunningham developed an interest in photography at the University of Washington in Seattle. Her earliest prints were made in the tradition of Pictorialism. She married etcher Roi Partridge in 1915, and the couple moved to San Francisco in 1917.

By the early 1920s Cunningham began to change her style, creating close-up, sharply detailed studies of plant life and other natural forms. Her experiments with form allied her with other Modernist photographers at the time, and in 1932 Cunningham joined the association of West Coast photographers known as Group f.64. Like other members of the group, she rejected the soft-focused sentimental subjects that were then popular in favour of images such as *Two Callas* (c. 1929), which conveys a sensuous delight in nature.

In the early 1930s, Cunningham worked briefly for *Vanity Fair* and produced images of entertainers and celebrities. After the breakup of Group f.64, she ran a portrait gallery and taught at several California art schools. A retrospective monograph, *Imogen! Imogen Cunningham Photographs, 1910–1973*, was published in 1974, and her final photographs were published in *After Ninety* in 1977. Cunningham died June 24, 1976, in San Francisco.

ALEKSANDR RODCHENKO

Born in St. Petersburg in 1891, Aleksandr Mikhailovich Rodchenko studied art at the Kazan School of Art in Odessa. He soon abandoned a Futurist style of painting in favour of a completely abstract, highly geometric style using a ruler and compass. His first major show was part of an exhibition organized in Moscow in 1916 by Vladimir Tatlin, and in 1918 Rodchenko presented a one-man show in Moscow. In the latter year he painted a series of black-on-black geometric paintings in response to the famous *White on White* painting of his rival, Kazimir Malevich. In 1919 Rodchenko began to make three-dimensional constructions out of wood, metal, and other materials, again using geometric shapes in dynamic compositions; some of these hanging sculptures were, in effect, mobiles.

Rodchenko led a wing of artists in the Constructivist movement—the Productivist group—who wanted to forge closer ties between the arts and industry and to produce works that they considered more appropriate in the daily lives of worker-consumers. He thus renounced easel painting in the 1920s and took up other art forms, among them photography; poster, book, and typographic design; furniture design; and stage and motion-picture set design. He held various government offices concerned with art-related projects, helped to establish art museums, and taught art. Rodchenko died on December 3, 1956, in Moscow.

LÁSZLÓ MOHOLY-NAGY

László Moholy-Nagy was born on July 20, 1895, in Bácsborsód, Hungary. After studying law and serving in World War I, he began to paint. He published Cubist-influenced woodcuts in a Hungarian avant-garde journal then went to Berlin, where from 1923 to 1929 he headed the metal workshop of the famous avant-garde school of design known as the Bauhaus. During his Bauhaus years Moholy-Nagy developed the theories of art education for which he is known. He created a widely accepted curriculum that focused on developing students' natural visual gifts instead of teaching them specialized skills.

As a painter and photographer Moholy-Nagy worked predominantly with light. He experimented with photograms, images composed by placing objects directly on light-sensitive paper, and he constructed "light-space modulators," oil paintings on transparent or polished surfaces that included mobile light effects.

After he left the Bauhaus in 1929, Moholy-Nagy became involved in stage design and filmmaking. Fleeing Nazi Germany in 1934, he went to Amsterdam and London, and in 1937 he moved to Chicago to organize the New Bauhaus, the first American school based on the Bauhaus program. He died November 24, 1946, in Chicago.

LEWIS HINE

Lewis Wickes Hine was born September 26, 1874, in Oshkosh, Wisconsin. Trained as a sociologist, he began to photograph the immigrants who crowded onto New York's Ellis Island in 1905. He also portrayed the tenements and sweatshops where the immigrants were forced to live and work.

In 1909 Hine published *Child Labor in the Carolinas* and *Day Laborers Before Their Time*, the first of his many photo stories documenting child labour. Two years later Hine was hired by the National Child Labor Committee to explore child-labour conditions in the United States more extensively. Hine traveled throughout the eastern half of the United States, gathering appalling pictures of exploited children and the slums in which they lived.

Late in World War I, Hine served as a photographer with the Red Cross. After the Armistice he remained with the Red Cross in the Balkans, and in 1919 he published the

Overseer supervising a girl operating a bobbin-winding machine at the Yazoo City Yarn Mills, Yazoo City, Mississippi, U.S., 1911; photograph by Lewis Hine.

photo story *The Children's Burden in the Balkans.*

After his return to New York City, Hine was hired to record the construction of the Empire State Building, then the tallest building in the world. To get the proper angle for certain pictures of the skyscraper, Hine had himself swung out over the city streets in a basket or bucket suspended from a crane or similar device. In 1932 these photographs were published as *Men at Work.* Thereafter he documented a number of government projects. Hine died November 3, 1940, in Hastings-on-Hudson, New York.

WALKER EVANS

Walker Evans was born on November 3, 1903, in St. Louis, Missouri. Following education on the east coast and at the Sorbonne in Paris, he settled in New York City to become a writer. He ended up turning to the camera. From mid-1935 to early 1937 Evans worked for the Farm Security Administration (FSA), photographing rural America.

In 1938 the Museum of Modern Art in New York City published *American Photographs* to accompany a retrospective exhibition of Evans's work to that time. The book's 87 pictures were made between 1929 and 1936 and selected by Evans. It is remarkable that more than a third of the pictures were made during the brief but astonishingly productive 18 months when Evans was employed by the FSA. *American Photographs* remains perhaps the most influential photography book of the modern era.

In 1943 Evans was hired by Time, Inc., and he spent the next 22 years with that publishing empire, most of them with the business magazine *Fortune*, with whom he developed a relationship as a photographer and writer that involved a comfortable salary, substantial independence, and little heavy lifting. He continued to photograph architecture, especially rural churches, and he also began a series of revealing, spontaneous photographs of people taken in the New York City subways.

During the 1940 and '50s—the heyday of photojournalism in the magazines—Evans, with his prickly, superior intelligence and jealously guarded independence, was not a useful role model for most working photographers. Yet, as the promise of the magazines began to lose its lustre, Evans increasingly became a hero to younger photographers who were not comfortable as part of an editorial team. Robert Frank, Garry Winogrand, Diane Arbus, and Lee Friedlander are among the most significant later photographers who have acknowledged their debt to Evans. His influence on artists in fields other than photography has also been great.

BERENICE ABBOT

Berenice Abbott was born July 17, 1898, in Springfield, Ohio. She worked as a darkroom assistant to Man Ray in Paris. In 1925 she set up her own photography studio in Paris and made several well-known portraits of expatriates, artists, writers, and aristocrats, including James Joyce, André Gide, Marcel Duchamp, Jean Cocteau, Max Ernst, Leo Stein, Peggy Guggenheim, and Edna St. Vincent Millay.

Abbott returned to New York City in 1929 and was struck by its rapid modernization. Continuing to do portraits, she also began to document the city itself. This project evolved into a Federal Art Project of the Works Progress Administration in 1935. Over the course of the next two decades Abbott taught photography at the New School for Social Research in New York and experimented with photography as a tool to illustrate scientific phenomena, such as magnetism and motion, for a mass audience. She also continued to document the landscape around her; for one project she photographed scenes along U.S. Route 1 from Florida to Maine. In 1968 she settled in Maine, where she concentrated on printing her work. Abbott died December 9, 1991, in Monson, Maine.

AUGUST SANDER

August Sander, born November 17, 1876, near Cologne, Germany, took up photography as a hobby and, after military service, pursued it professionally. After his army service in World War I, he settled permanently in Cologne, where in the 1920s his circle of friends included photographers and painters dedicated to what was called Neue Sachlichkeit, or New Objectivity.

After photographing local farmers near Cologne, Sander was inspired to produce a series of portraits of German people from all strata of society. His portraits were usually stark, photographed straight on in natural light, with facts of the sitters' class and profession alluded to through clothing, gesture, and backdrop. He published *Antlitz der Zeit* (*Face of Our Time*), the first of what was projected to be a series offering a sociological, pictorial survey of the class structure of Germany.

When the Nazis came to power in 1933, Sander was subjected to official disapproval, perhaps because of the natural, almost vulnerable manner in which he showed the people of Germany or perhaps because of the heterogeneity it revealed. The plates for *Antlitz der Zeit* were seized and destroyed. (One of Sander's sons, a socialist, was jailed and died in prison.) During this period Sander turned to less-controversial rural landscapes and nature subjects.

The Federal Republic of Germany awarded Sander the Order of Merit in 1960. He died April 20, 1964, in Cologne.

ROBERT DOISNEAU

Robert Doisneau was born on April 14, 1912, in Gentilly, France. As a young man he attended the École Estienne in Paris, but he always claimed that the streets of the working class neighbourhood of Gentilly provided his most important schooling. He began photographing just as Modernist ideas were beginning to promote photography as the prime medium for advertising and reportage. Doisneau first worked for the advertising photographer André Vigneau, in whose studio he met artists and writers with avant-garde ideas, and then during the Depression years of the 1930s he worked as an industrial photographer for the Renault car company. He also photographed in the streets and neighbourhoods of Paris, hoping to sell work to the picture magazines, which were expanding their use of photographs as illustration.

With his career interrupted by World War II and the German occupation, Doisneau became a member of the resistance, using his métier to provide forged documents for the underground. In 1945 he recommenced his advertising and magazine work, including fashion photography and reportage for Vogue magazine from 1948 to 1952.

In the 1950s Doisneau also became active in Group XV, an organization of photographers devoted to improving both the artistry and technical aspects of photography. From then on, he photographed a vast array of people and events, often juxtaposing conformist and maverick elements in images marked by an exquisite sense of humour, by antiestablishment values, and, above all, by his deeply felt humanism. He died April 1, 1994, in Broussais, France.

BRASSAÏ

The photographer known as Brassaï, was born Gyula Halász on September 9, 1899, in Brassó,

Transylvania. In Paris, he associated with such artists as Pablo Picasso, Joan Miró, Salvador Dalí, and the writer Henry Miller. An artist who disliked photography at first, he found it necessary to use it in his journalistic assignments and soon came to appreciate the medium's unique aesthetic qualities.

Brassaï's early photographs concentrated on the nighttime world of Montparnasse, a district of Paris then noted for its artists, streetwalkers, and petty criminals. His pictures were published in several successful books, bringing him international fame and a hint of scandal. Many of Brassaï's postwar pictures continued the themes and techniques of his early work. In these photographs Brassaï preferred static over active subjects, but he imbued even the most inanimate images with a warm sense of human life.

The Museum of Modern Art in New York City held a retrospective exhibition of Brassaï's work in 1968, and several books of his work were published in his later years. Brassaï died July 8, 1984, near Nice, France.

ERICH SALOMON

Erich Salomon was born April 28, 1886, in Berlin, Germany. He began practicing law but became a freelance photographer when he bought an Ermanox, one of the first miniature cameras equipped with a high-speed lens, which enabled him to photograph in dim light. He concealed this camera in an attaché case and secretly took photographs of a sensational murder trial. These sold so well to news periodicals that he became a professional photojournalist. He began to specialize in photographing international conferences and social gatherings of heads of state, with the intention of showing the human qualities of world leaders who were usually only captured in stiff, formal portraits. Working inconspicuously, he especially enjoyed catching the leaders' unguarded moments of fatigue, delight, or disgust. Salomon's informal, spontaneous style had a lasting influence on the way photojournalists captured famous figures.

Because he was Jewish, Salomon went into hiding in the Netherlands during World War II, but he was finally betrayed by a Dutch Nazi. In May 1944 he was sent to the concentration camp at Auschwitz, where he died.

ROBERT CAPA

Robert Capa was born Friedmann Endre Ernö, in 1913, in Budapest, Hungary. He first achieved fame as a war correspondent in the Spanish Civil War. By 1936 his mature style fully emerged in grim, close-up views of death such as *Loyalist Soldier, Spain*. Such immediate images embodied Capa's famous saying, "If your pictures aren't good enough, then you aren't close enough." In World War II he covered much of the heaviest fighting in Africa, Sicily, and Italy for *Life* magazine, and his photographs of the Normandy Invasion became some of the most memorable of the war.

In 1947 Capa joined with the Henri Cartier-Bresson and David ("Chim") Seymour to found Magnum Photos, the first cooperative agency of international freelance photographers. Although he covered the fighting in Palestine in 1948, most of Capa's time was spent guiding newer members of Magnum and selling their work. He served as the director of the Magnum office in Paris from 1950 to 1953. In 1954 Capa volunteered to photograph the French Indochina War for *Life* and was killed by a land mine while on assignment. His untimely death helped establish his posthumous reputation as a quintessentially fearless photojournalist.

ALFRED EISENSTADT

Born in Poland on December 6, 1898, Alfred Eisenstaedt served in the German army in World War I from 1916 to 1918, sustaining injuries in both legs. He became an enthusiastic amateur photographer, turning professional in 1929 and joining the lively photojournalism scene in Germany. During the 1920s and early '30s he was especially influenced by Erich Salomon.

Eisenstaedt was particularly skilled in the use of the 35-mm Leica camera. His work, often created in this format, had appeared in many European picture magazines by the early 1930s. He covered the rise of Adolf Hitler and in 1935 created a notable series of photographs of Ethiopia, just before the Italian invasion. That same year he immigrated to the United States, and in April 1936 he became one of the first four photographers hired by the new picture magazine *Life*, where he eventually had some 2,500 photo-essays and 90 cover photos featured.

Eisenstaedt photographed kings, dictators, and motion picture stars, but he also sensitively portrayed ordinary people in workaday situations. His aim, he once said, was "to find and catch the storytelling moment." He died August 23, 1995, in Oak Bluffs, Massachusetts.

WEEGEE

On June 12, 1899, Usher Fellig was born in Austria-Hungary, now Poland. Renamed Arthur when his family immigrated to the United States, he eventually took a job in the darkroom of Acme Newspictures and later worked as a freelance newspaper photographer. His uncanny ability to appear with his camera at crime scenes as the police arrived—or sometimes even before—led to the moniker "Weegee," a phonetic spelling of the first word in Ouija board, a device used in occultism to receive messages from the spirit world.

For much of his career, Weegee was, in his own words, "spellbound by the mystery of murder." His images have the air of a still from a film noir, photographed as they were usually at night and often with infrared film and flash. He paid special attention to the expressions and gestures of his subjects, who for the most part came from the lower strata of New York society. His feelings about privileged New Yorkers were typified in a photograph entitled *The Critic*, in which an ill-clothed onlooker hisses at two bejeweled women attending the opera.

From 1947 to 1952 Weegee lived in Hollywood, acting as technical advisor, playing bit parts in a few films, and photographing material that was published in 1953 as *Naked Hollywood.* In 1961 his autobiography, *Weegee by Weegee*, was published. Weegee died in New York City on December 26, 1968. His uncanny ability to capture a dramatic segment of New York street life remains his most significant contribution to photography.

CHAPTER FOUR

CONTEMPORARY PHOTOGRAPHY: 1945-PRESENT

With the improvement in colour materials and processes, photographers became more interested in its creative possibilities.

POSTWAR DEVELOPMENTS

Beginning in the 1940s, American photographer Eliot Porter produced subtle studies of birds and nature in which colour allowed him to render an unparalleled level of nuance. Appreciated for both their scientific and their aesthetic value, these photographs embodied the potential of colour. Austrian photojournalist Ernst Haas first used colour in the photo-essay *New York* for *Life* magazine in 1953. Through this and similar projects he challenged the standard of using only black and white in photojournalism, and his use of colour added vibrancy to images of everyday life. While these and other experiments achieved some success, it was not until later in the century that colour dominated photographic output and was incorporated into daily newspapers.

ABSTRACT EXPRESSIONIST INFLUENCES

In the period after World War II, as the United States entered a period of domestic peace and prosperity, many photographers there moved away from documentary realities and focused instead on the intrinsic qualities of photography; such experiments paralleled the ascendancy of the Abstract Expressionist art movement, which similarly looked at the intrinsic quality of painting.

Minor White combined ideas about photography's incomparable

Minor White was interested in the spiritual content of photography.

descriptive power, taken from Edward Weston, with those about its emotional expressiveness, taken from Alfred Stieglitz. Through his long career as an influential teacher and founding editor of *Aperture*, White developed the idea that a photograph should contain an inner message that might not be immediately visible on the surface.

MINOR WHITE

Minor White (1908–1976) was an American photographer and editor whose efforts to extend photography's range of expression greatly influenced creative photography in the mid-20th century.

White took up photography while very young but set it aside for a number of years to study botany and, later, poetry. He began to photograph seriously in 1937. His early years as a photographer were spent working for the Works Progress Administration (WPA) in Portland, Oregon Many WPA photographers were chiefly concerned with documentation; White, however, preferred a more personal approach. Several of his photographs were included in a show at the Museum of Modern Art in New York City in 1941.

White served in the U.S. Army during World War II, and in 1945 he moved to New York City, where he became part of a circle of friends that included the influential photographers Edward Steichen and Alfred Stieglitz. His contact with Stieglitz helped him discover his own distinctive style. From Stieglitz he learned the expressive potential of the sequence, a group of photographs presented as a unit. White would present his work in such units along with text, creating arrangements that he hoped would inspire different moods, emotions, and associations in the viewer, moving beyond the conventional expressive possibilities of still photography. White also learned from Stieglitz the idea of the "equivalent," or a photographic image intended as a visual metaphor for a state of being. Both in his photographs and in his writing, White became the foremost exponent of the sequence and the equivalent.

In 1946 White moved to San Francisco, where he worked closely with the photographer Ansel Adams. Adams's zone system, a method of visualizing how the scene or object to be photographed will appear in the final print, formed another major influence on White's work. The next year White succeeded

(continued on the next page)

(continued from the previous page)

Adams as director of the photography department of the California School of Fine Arts. During this period he also befriended photographer Edward Weston. Already a meticulous technician who was scrupulously faithful in his work to the tones and textures of nature, White was inspired by Weston's use of realism and tonal beauty in photographic prints. Always interested in the spiritual content of photography, White followed aspects of Zen philosophy and often gave mystical interpretations to his work.

In 1952 he returned to New York City and became editor of the influential photography magazine *Aperture*, which he and others founded that year, and *Image*, the journal of George Eastman House, which he edited from 1953 to 1957.

White traveled throughout the United States in the late 1950s and early '60s and began to experiment with colour photographs. In 1965 he settled in Cambridge, Massachusetts, and became professor of creative photography at the Massachusetts Institute of Technology. Among his best-known books are two collections, *Mirrors, Messages, Manifestations* (1969), which features some of his sequences, and *Minor White: Rites and Passages* (1978), with excerpts from his diaries and letters and a biographical essay by James Baker Hall.

Other American photographers influenced by the Abstract Expressionist style of the era included Aaron Siskind, who found formal configurations in graffiti, weathered wood and plaster, and torn billboards (what he called the "detritus of the world"), and Harry Callahan, whose work demonstrated a highly developed sense of linear form. Siskind and Callahan inspired a generation of young photographers through their teachings at the Institute of Design, the school that had been started in 1937 in Chicago by Moholy-Nagy as the New Bauhaus. Barbara Crane, Ken Josephson, and Garry Winogrand were among students who later achieved fame. In England Bill Brandt created expressive photographs of nudes, shooting his subject matter at such close range that the human body took on the appearance of series of patterns and abstract designs. In Germany Otto Steinert led the Fotoform group of photographers, who created close-up views of nature that were also nearly abstract in their effects.

By the 1960s similar styles and ideas in photography had spread to Asia, in part because photographic magazines became widely available. Japanese photographers had been aware of Modernist currents before World War II, but afterward they pursued them more openly. Among the important photographers of this generation were Shōmei Tomatsu, who made vivid images on the streets of Tokyo; Eikō Hosoe, who captured imagery evoking human sensuality; and Hiroshi Sugimoto, who was entranced by images conveying stillness and emptiness. For a period the government in China exerted control over photographic imagery, but by the late 20th century photographers had found some freedoms. Chen Changfen was able to indulge his interest in colour abstractions, and Xie Hailong produced photographic documentations of problems in contemporary Chinese society, such as the difficulties faced by rural students seeking an education.

STREET PHOTOGRAPHY

Street photography might be considered a special aspect of documentation: the street photographer is intrigued by the serendipitous nature of street activity, but, in contrast to the social documentarian, the street photographer does not necessarily have a social purpose in mind. The very publicness of the setting enables the photographer to take candid pictures of strangers, often without their knowledge. Street photographers prefer to isolate and capture moments which might otherwise go unnoticed.

By the close of the war and throughout the late 1940s and '50s, William Klein, Lisette Model, Helen Levitt, Roy DeCarava, and Robert Frank were making careers of documenting American culture. The photographs they took were provocative and often contained vulgar or unaesthetic subject matter. Levitt was drawn to the poor neighbourhoods of New York City, where she often photographed children playing in the streets. DeCarava chronicled African American life in Harlem and the great jazz musicians of the postwar period, becoming the first African American photographer whose work embodied the spirit of true street photography. His shadowy pictures of everyday life in Harlem

Street photographer Roy DeCarava chronicled daily life in Harlem.

were a revelation from an insider's point of view. Klein and Model used an aggressive style on the street, confronting subjects head-on with their cameras. The street photographers of that period, to a lesser or greater degree, all challenged the prevailing "straight photography" aesthetic, which, since the turn of the century, had urged the use of basic camera capabilities and photographic processes in the darkroom. They instead photographed from unconventional perspectives and produced grainy prints that contained blurry forms in motion.

Frank introduced a new kind of photographic documentation, one that placed greater value on images that evoked emotion and subjectivity. Departing from the most basic of traditional photographic methods, he often took photos without even looking through the viewfinder. He preferred leaving it to chance instead, welcoming imperfections and ambiguity. For that reason, it was hard to create a single perfect masterpiece, which had been the aim of many of his peers and predecessors, especially Cartier-Bresson. Frank wanted to express his perspective through a sequence of photographs, almost like the stream-of-consciousness technique of prose writers. The desire to offer more of a visual narrative experience worked best in book form, and it can be seen to great advantage in his groundbreaking and highly influential book *The Americans* (1959; first published in Paris in 1958), controversial for its dark perspective and critical view of humanity. *The Americans* and Frank paved the way for new forms of expression, new formats of display, and an artistic freedom among photographers that endured into the 21st century.

Outside of the United States, Robert Doisneau was documenting life on the streets of Paris during the postwar period. Compared with his American counterparts, Doisneau had a light touch, teasing out more casual everyday moments rather than bizarre and disturbing ones. The style was popular elsewhere as well. Notable among the street photographers in other parts of the world at that time and through the end of the 20th century were Manuel Álvarez Bravo and his student Graciela Iturbide in Mexico, Bill Brandt in London, and Josef Koudelka in Czechoslovakia.

Joel Meyerowitz, Garry Winogrand, Lee Friedlander, and Diane Arbus were notable American street photographers of the 1960s

VIVIAN MAIER

Born in the United States in 1926, Vivian Maier, spent much of her childhood in France and likely became interested in photography

(continued on the next page)

(continued from the previous page)

at an early age. Her first photos were taken in France in the late 1940s with a Kodak Brownie camera. She returned to the United States in 1951, first living in New York City and in 1956 moving to Highland Park, a northern suburb of Chicago, to accept a job as a nanny for a family, with whom she stayed until the early 1970s.

Maier photographed the urban human landscape over the course of three decades. Her preferred subjects were children, the poor, the marginalized, and the elderly, some of them aware of her and some not. She also made a number of self-portraits. She worked in a black-and-white documentary style until the early 1970s, when she took up colour and also began to adopt a more abstract approach.

Though contradictory biographical details appear in sources that tell her story, it is clear from interviews with her employers and their children that she was an intensely private person with few, if any, friends. She chose to keep her work to herself. In addition to her tens of thousands of photographic materials, Maier collected found objects throughout her life and saved an extraordinarily vast trove of belongings in the two storage lockers she rented. Those artifacts of her life were used to help reconstruct her biography.

In 2007, two years before her death, Maier's belongings were collected from a storage unit sold for nonpayment. Hundreds of thousands of negatives, prints, rolls of film, home movies, and audio interviews were auctioned off to several buyers. The privatization of her materials in this way raised legal, academic, and ethical questions about the posthumous use, profit from, and analysis of her work. Given that virtually none of the work by Maier that is being published and exhibited was processed or printed by the artist herself, one of the critical questions is of her personal aesthetic and artistic vision.

and '70s. Though they looked to Frank for inspiration, they each shaped a personal and distinctive style that favoured realism over beauty. The influence of Atget is apparent in Friedlander's photographs of urban life across the United States, though his images of reflections in storefront windows have a decidedly more depressed tone than those of Atget. Winogrand's crowded and theatrical scenes on New York City streets captured the crazy chaos of the world with immediacy and energy unlike any other street photographer. Arbus unflinchingly examined the marginalized figures of society. Her dramatic straightforward images awkwardly bring to the fore figures who were often shunted to the background, avoided, or ignored in daily life.

In 1967 photography scholar and curator John Szarkowski organized the now-celebrated exhibition *New Documents* at the Museum of Modern Art in New York City, featuring the work of Arbus, Friedlander, and Winogrand and identifying them as the new generation of photographers following in the footsteps of Frank

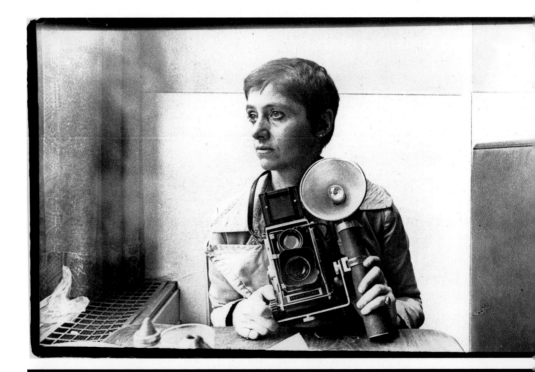

Diane Arbus focused her lens on marginalized parts of society not often featured in photography.

and inspired by the "snapshot" look. Szarkowski's exhibition revealed as much about the fascinations of the people behind the camera as those in front of it, and some critics found the work to be voyeuristic and exploitative. Whatever its merits and flaws, *New Documents* defined a new form of documentary photography, which marked a shift in the notion of documentation as strictly objective and also in the perception of the art of photography itself: for the first time in the history of photography, the photographer was clearly revealed as an artist with a point of view and not a mere recorder of facts.

The generations of photographers that followed were greatly influenced by the personal approach. Photographers of the late 20th and early 21st centuries who took the street as a central focus include Raghubir Singh, Bruce Gilden, Martin Parr, Mary Ellen Mark, Jeff Mermelstein, Sylvia Plachy, Mitch Epstein, Alex Webb, Melanie Einzig, and Philip-Lorca diCorcia.

PUSHING THE LIMITS OF SOCIAL DOCUMENTATION

Other social documentation in the postwar period used the medium to examine contemporary society from a distance. Such efforts had various labels, including "social landscape." Inspired by Swiss-born émigré Robert Frank, who during the 1950s viewed American culture with an ironic eye, American photographers such as Bruce Davidson, Lee Friedlander, and William Klein were among those whose work suggested the effects of contemporary culture on people in industrialized societies. Often utilizing 35-mm cameras, these photographers caught seeming mundane everyday moments in works that resembled snapshots. Beneath this seeming spontaneity lay an element of critique, however, that in some cases paralleled Pop Art's examination of the banality of contemporary consumer culture.

Several important photographers defied categorization. In the early 1960s the photographer Sedou Keïta, working as a commercial portraitist in Mali, allowed his sitters to arrange and costume themselves. The resulting photographs created an extensive and compelling documentation of his country's people. In the same period, influenced by the mordant eye of the earlier Austrian émigré photographer Lisette Model, Diane Arbus created challenging portraits of people living outside prescribed ideas of "normalcy," such as transvestites and the mentally ill.

DEVELOPMENTS FROM THE 1970S TO THE PRESENT

Continuing the example set by Diane Arbus, a gritty sort of social documentation emerged beginning in the 1970s and '80s, when photographers such as Larry Clark and Nan Goldin documented alternative lifestyles involving drug addiction, transvestism, and casual sex. In particular, Goldin created an elaborate series entitled *The Ballad of Sexual Dependency*, sometimes accompanied by music and spoken work, through which she created an evolving record of the people she and her camera encountered. Such direct, unflinching photographs established intimate documentary work as an important genre in the late 20th century. Photographers such as Sally Mann and Tina Barney extended this genre to portray intimate, sometimes unsettling images of their own families.

Goldin and Clark both usually photographed in colour, which added to the harsh sense of reality in their work; this represented a general move toward colour among photographers of their generation. William Eggleston pushed the artistic boundaries of colour by using it to explore the banality of small-town existence; along these same lines, Candida Höfer used colour to emphasize the tedium of institutional life. Richard Misrach created a massive project, known as the *Desert Cantos*, in which he photographed desert scenes in colour, sometimes juxtaposed against sinister elements such as

William Eggleston explored the banality of small-town life, as in this photograph of an abandoned tricycle on a neighborhood street.

nuclear sites. Barbara Norfleet, Joel Meyerowitz, Stephen Shore, Barbara Kasten, and Franco Fontana were among the other prominent photographers of the period who used colour expressively in landscapes, interiors, still lifes, and street scenes.

From the 1970s on, as the advent of television news began to affect the popularity of picture magazines, many photojournalists whose work had been published in magazines began to take advantage of a burgeoning interest in photographic picture books. These, often produced in conjunction with exhibits, comprised photographs of newsworthy events or topics of social interest along with informative texts. Working in black and white, Swiss-born photographer Claudia Andujar (working in Brazil) and Mexican photographer Graciela Iturbide portrayed indigenous peoples—groups they believed were becoming marginalized by society—and their customs. Other important figures included English photographer Don McCullin, who portrayed the devastation brought about by wars in Vietnam and in Africa; French photojournalist Raymond Depardon, who worked in Asia, Africa, and Europe; American Mary Ellen Mark, who photographed street performers and prostitutes in India, depicted street children in Seattle, Washington, and spent time documenting the inmates of a mental hospital; and Brazilian photographer Sebastião Salgado, who examined work and workers throughout the world, exhibiting and publishing a number of books on that topic. For his ability to make world events come pictorially alive, American James Nachtwey was three times the winner of the International Center of Photography's photojournalism awards. By the end of the century, the technology used by these photojournalists had changed. Digital cameras sent images directly to computers, and programs allowed images to be altered seamlessly, making newspaper and magazine darkrooms obsolete.

CINEMATOGRAPHY

The earliest motion pictures were filmed as if they were stage plays, using just one or a few cameras in static frontal photography. By the second and third decades of the 20th century, however, in the hands of such cameramen as Billy Bitzer (working with director D.W. Griffith) the camera was doing close-ups, shooting from moving vehicles, employing backlighting and other lighting effects, and generally being used in ways that separated the motion picture from theatrical tradition. With the coming of sound, the inventive motion was interrupted when the noisy cameras were perforce made stationary in sound-proof enclosures not easily moved, but the development of silent cameras again made cinematography flexible. The development of the camera crane (first used in 1929) also expanded the camera's vision, as did the use of wider-angle lenses to achieve a greater depth of field (as Gregg Toland did in the impressive scenes of *Citizen Kane* [1941]).The two most important events in cinematography after the coming of sound were undoubtedly colour and wide-screen processes. Also important are advances in special effects, as developed in Stanley Kubrick's *2001: A Space Odyssey* (1968), with cameraman Geoffrey Unsworth, and in George Lucas's *Star Wars* (1977), with cinematographers Gilbert Taylor and (for special effects) John Dykstra.

The differences between photography and cinematography are many. A single photograph may be a complete work in itself, but a cinematographer deals with relations between shots and between groups of shots. A main character, for instance, may initially come on screen unrecognizable in shadows and near-darkness (as Orson Welles did in *The Third Man* [1949]); as a single shot, it might be poor photography, but cinematographically it leads into other shots that reveal the man and give the movie style and integration. Cinematography is also far more collaborative than photography.The cinematographer must plan his work with the producer, the director, the designer, the sound

(continued on the next page)

(continued from the previous page)

technicians, and each of the actors. The camera crew itself may be complex, especially in a feature film; the chief cinematographer supervises a second cameraman (or camera operator), who handles the camera; an assistant operator (the focus-puller), whose main function is to adjust the focusing; an assistant known as the clapper-loader, or clapper boy, who holds up the slate at the beginning of the shot, loads the magazines with film, and keeps a record of the footage and other details; and the "grips," who carry or push around equipment and lay tracks for the camera dolly. The cinematographer may also be in charge of the gaffer, or chief electrician (a lighting technician), who is assisted by one or more "best boys." A big-budget film may have additionally a special-effects crew and sometimes a whole second unit of cinematographer and assistants.

ARCHITECTURE AND THE BUILT ENVIRONMENT

The documentation of artifacts, begun in the 19th century, continued to interest late 20th-century photographers. Italian photographer Gabriele Basilico and American photographer Lewis Baltz concentrated on architecture and the built environment. The German duo Bernd and Hilla Becher produced an extensive portrayal of industrial buildings such as mine tipples and factories, which they usually displayed in carefully planned arrangements of multiple prints. This sort of project combined traditional documentary conventions with postmodern concepts about typologies.

Fashion photographers found their role redefined at the end of the century. As giants of fashion photography from earlier in the century such as Irving Penn and Richard Avedon became the subjects of major museum retrospectives, fashion and celebrity photography, initially meant to illustrate fashion magazines such as *Harper's Bazaar* and *Vogue*, became fully recognized as an art form. Photographers David LaChapelle, Annie Leibovitz, Helmut Newton, Mario Testino, and Bruce Weber were among those whose work was esteemed enough to be exhibited in both gallery and museum shows and published in popular monographs.

Throughout most of the 20th century, the art world was dominated by painting and sculpture, with photography seen as a separate but not necessarily equal art form. In the 1980s and '90s, however, as new media such as video, performance, and installation blurred definitions of "art," photography became one of the art world's most prominent media. During this period a generation of prominent photographers, many of them American,

Richard Avedon photographs fashion model Jean Shrimpton at this 1965 photo shoot.

helped break down these barriers between photography and "art." American Robert Mapplethorpe received a maelstrom of attention for his masterfully executed photographs, which ranged from still lifes to portraits to, most controversially, sadomasochistic and homo-erotic themes. American photographer Cindy Sherman became an international art star for her elaborately staged self-portraits in which she posed in a variety of stereotypical feminine roles and, in so doing, critiqued these clichés. Barbara Kruger, also American, gained promi-nence for her modern-day montages, in which she juxtaposed photographic images with text containing social critique—perhaps most famously, the phrases "I Shop, Therefore I Am" and "Your Body Is a Battleground." A similar use of photography in mixed-media was pursued by American Carrie Mae Weems, who repro-duced 19th-century photographs of slaves on a series of banners and scrims, presenting them in a three-dimensional arrangement that commented on the visual representation of African Americans throughout history.

At the turn of the 21st century, the wiz-ardry made possible by digital capabilities was reflected in the work of a prominent new generation of international photogra-phers. Most of these photographers worked almost exclusively in colour; indeed, at the turn of the century, black-and-white prints of contemporary photographic work were the exception rather than the rule, as new com-puter programs made possible a vast array of colours, many of which may not have existed at the time of the actual exposure.

Cindy Sherman's "disguised" self-portraits comment on social role-playing and sexual stereotypes.

Computers also allowed photographers to combine their photographs with other digitally captured or scanned images and to make works on an unprecedented scale. Major figures at the turn of the century, all of whom worked on a large scale, included German photographer Andreas Gursky, known for his detached views of spaces such as stock exchanges and government buildings; German photographer Thomas Struth, whose work dispassionately captured the interiors of museum galleries; Japanese photographer Mariko Mori, who featured herself as a character in candy-coloured futuristic landscapes; and British photographer Sam Taylor-Wood, who created panoramic scenes of interiors filled with bored, isolated-seeming subjects. Exhibited in venues formerly reserved for painting, and at times along with paintings, monumental photographs by this new generation of photographers effectively ushered in a new era of possibility for the medium.

NOTABLE FIGURES IN CONTEMPORARY PHOTOGRAPHY

Since the list of important photographers of the 20th century and beyond is long and varied, the following discussion draws biographical sketches of just some of history's most influential.

ELIOT PORTER

Eliot Porter (1901–1990) was an American photographer noted for his detailed and exquisite colour images of birds and landscapes.

Porter, the brother of painter Fairfield Porter, trained as an engineer at Harvard College (B.S., 1924) and as a physician at Harvard Medical School (M.D., 1929). He taught biochemistry at Harvard from 1929 to 1939, when he turned his hobby of photographing birds into a career. Photographer Alfred Stieglitz praised his work and gave him a show at his An American Place gallery in 1939. Porter's early photographs of birds were in black and white, but in the early 1940s he began using the then-new Kodachrome colour film, whose slow speed required the use of large flashbulbs in order to achieve correct exposures. Porter worked with a cumbersome large-format camera, valuing the greater detail this equipment allowed. Lacking mobility because of the size of his camera and its reliance on large flashbulbs, Porter often had to spend hours and even days waiting for specific birds to perch near him. His bird photographs, much like the paintings and drawings of John James Audubon, are ornithologically important because of their meticulous detail while also artistically of note because of their fine technique and composition. His work was in the style of Ansel Adams's "straight" photography, showing the subject in a straightforward manner, with an emphasis on tone and detail.

Gradually Porter's colour photography shifted from the portrayal of birds to natural landscapes, which he first presented in 1962 in an exhibition entitled "In Wildness Is the Preservation of the World," with an accompanying catalog. Porter was active in the cause of environmental preservation and had this and other books published by the Sierra Club. He published many other collections of nature photographs, including those in *The Place No One Knew* (1963), *Baja California* (1967), *Galapagos* (1968), *Appalachian Wilderness* (1970), and *The Tree Where Man Was Born* (1972). Many of his finest photographs of birds were collected *in Birds of North America* (1972).

BILL BRANDT

Bill Brandt (1904–1983) was known principally for his documentation of 20th-century British life and for his unusual nudes. Brandt briefly worked in the Paris studio of Man Ray then returned to England to become a freelance photojournalist, producing a series of photographs depicting the daily life of all strata of English society. Many of these photographs reveal the influence of Eugène Atget, Brassaï, and Henri Cartier-Bresson, all of whom similarly documented their immediate surroundings.

In the late 1930s, Brandt began to photograph the industrial cities and coal-mining districts of northern England, creating images that reveal the desperation of England's industrial workers during the 1930s. When World War

II began, Brandt became a staff photographer for the British Home Office, capturing home-front scenes such as Londoners crowded into air-raid shelters in the city's underground train stations.

After the war Brandt photographed a series of landscapes associated with English literature. His work in the 1950s became increasingly expressionistic. In one series he placed his extremely wide-angle fixed-focus camera at close range to the human body; this caused distortion and transformed the human figure into a series of abstract designs. In other photographs from this time, however, Brandt made the distorted human form become an integral element of a stark landscape of cliffs and rocky beach.

BERND AND HILLA BECHER

Bernd Becher (1931–2007) and Hilla Becher (1934–) were born in Germany. They met in Düsseldorf and married in 1961. The Bechers' photographs established a signature style from their earliest work and continued in that mode for nearly 50 years. By choosing a fixed vantage point from which to capture the elements of the industrial landscape, the Bechers strove to eliminate any trace of subjectivity in their compositions. In order to avoid shadows, they photographed on cloudy days, lending their images an airless and expressionless quality.

The cumulative effect of their method was a straightforward reductive image of the geometry of their subject.

The couple had strong views regarding preservation and hoped that their documentation would serve as the memory of the quickly forgotten and the obsolete. They photographed industrial structures in Germany and throughout Europe, as well as in many regions of North America. Within the photography field, the Bechers became associated with a new flock of artists working in reaction to the romantic landscape aesthetic. Their new version of the American landscape—a radical departure from the traditional photographic landscape by artists such as Ansel Adams— drew attention to a new, somewhat troubling, understanding of the relationship between the individual and nature.

The Bechers' sharply focused "objective" style of documentation found its source in the Neue Sachlichkeit ("New Objectivity") movement, which had emerged in Germany in the 1920s. The group, which included photographers such as August Sander, Karl Blossfeldt, and Albert Renger-Patzsch, rejected the sentimentality of Pictorialism, a school of photography then losing momentum, which emphasized the beautiful, painterly, and well-composed image. Together the Bechers established a photography department in 1976 at the Staatliche Kunstakademie in

Düsseldorf. They influenced many contemporary photographers, and Bernd taught four of the best-known photographers to emerge from Germany in the late 20th century: Thomas Struth, Thomas Ruff, Candida Höfer, and Andreas Gursky. Their styles were so distinctive and their careers so successful that they came to be known as the Düsseldorf School of Photography.

WILLIAM EGGLESTON

Born in 1939 in Memphis, Tennessee, William Eggleston was influenced by the photography of Walker Evans and Henri Cartier-Bresson early in his life. In 1964, he began to experiment in colour photography, which had rarely been appreciated as fine art. Sensing an opportunity to forge new ground, he set to capture images he encountered in his surroundings with a neutral eye—devoid of either sentiment or irony—and, radically, in full colour. Over the next decade, he produced thousands of photographs, focusing on ordinary Americans and the landscapes and structures. In the early 1970s Eggleston discovered that printing with a dye-transfer process, a practice common in high-end advertising, would allow him to control the colours of his photographs and thereby heighten their effect.

The recipient of a Guggenheim fellowship in 1974, Eggleston received an additional career boost two years later with a solo exhibition at New York City's Museum of Modern Art. The show provoked hostility from some critics who judged the snapshotlike pictures banal and lacking in artistry. Other viewers, however, found that Eggleston's intensely saturated hues and striking perspectives imbued an ominous or dreamlike quality to their seemingly mundane subjects. He soon took on various commissioned projects, many in the southern United States.

By the turn of the 21st century, the skepticism that had initially greeted Eggleston's work had largely dissipated, and the retrospective "William Eggleston: Democratic Camera, Photographs and Videos, 1961–2008" solidified his reputation as a skilled innovator.

GORDON PARKS

Gordon Parks (born 1912–2006) grew up in poverty, the son of a tenant farmer. A high school dropout, he bought a camera and initially made a name for himself as a portrait and fashion photographer. After moving to Chicago, he began chronicling life on the city's impoverished South Side. These photographs led to a Julius Rosenwald Fellowship, and in 1942 he became a photographer at the Farm Security Administration (FSA). While with the FSA, he took perhaps his best-known photograph, *American Gothic*, which featured an African American cleaning woman holding a mop and broom while standing in front of an American flag.

In 1948 Parks became the first African American staff photographer for *Life* magazine. He became known for his portrayals of ghetto life, black nationalists, and the civil rights movement. A photo-essay about a child from a Brazilian slum was expanded into a television documentary (1962). Parks also was noted for his intimate portraits of such public figures as Ingrid Bergman, Barbra Streisand, Gloria Vanderbilt, and Muhammad Ali.

Parks also authored works of fiction, poetry, and essays. In 1968 he became the first African American to direct a major motion picture, writing, producing, and scoring the film as well. His next effort, *Shaft* (1971), helped give rise to the genre of African American action films known as "blaxploitation."

GARRY WINOGRAND

Garry Winogrand (1928–1984) became interested in photography while studying painting at Columbia University. At the New School for Social Research, he was encouraged by Alexey Brodovitch to rely on instinct rather than science and methodical technique when photographing, advice that had a significant impact on Winogrand's approach to his craft.

Winogrand's aesthetic vision began to emerge in 1960, when he took to the streets of New York City with his Leica camera and his bravado and began using a wide-angle lens to create lyrical photographs of the human condition. Taking cues from documentary photographers Walker Evans and Robert Frank—the latter of whom was getting attention for his grainy candid photos—Winogrand taught himself how to tilt the camera with the wide-angle lens in such a way that allowed him to include elements that, given his close vantage point, would have otherwise been cut off by the frame. This practice also resulted in unusual compositions with a certain amount of distortion. Shooting many frames in quick succession, Winogrand did not strive for the classical composition of traditional photography. The tilted-frame technique, as opposed to placing the horizon line parallel to the frame, was Winogrand's (successful) experiment and subsequently became common practice among street photographers. His style quickly acquired the name "snapshot aesthetic," a term Winogrand rejected because it implied that his approach was casual and without focus.

His photographs of people in public places and on the streets of New York and, later, Los Angeles, were tinged with humour and satire. During the latter period of his life, he photographed obsessively and did not edit even a fraction of the thousands of rolls of film that he shot.

Winogrand died suddenly at age 56, six weeks after he was diagnosed with cancer. He left a body of work that was in complete disarray. Winogrand's frenetic style captured the chaos of life with immediacy and energy and left an indelible mark on 20th-century photography. His archive, most of which is held at the Center for Creative Photography at the University of Arizona, continued to yield new unprinted work for decades after his death. The first major retrospective of Winogrand's work in 25 years, held at the San Francisco Museum of Modern Art in 2013, exhibited nearly 100 photos that the photographer himself had never seen.

LISETTE MODEL

Viennese photographer Lisette Model (1901–1983) began as a music student to the avant-garde composer Arnold Schoenberg. In Paris in 1926 she came into contact with other émigré artists, including the photographers Rogi André and Florence Henri and possibly Berenice Abbott. About 1933 she abandoned all efforts to pursue a career in music and she turned to photography as a means of earning a living. In 1934 Model produced *Promenade des Anglais*, a series of startling, satiric portraits of the idle rich. These images established Model as a master photographer and they remain among her most often reproduced images.

She married Russian-born painter Evsa Model in 1937, and a year later the couple immigrated to New York City. Stimulated by the city's energy, Model embarked on a new phase of photography, making images of street activity and reflections in store windows, as well as portraits of celebrities, entertainers, and street people. Her work appeared in exhibitions at the Museum of Modern Art in New York City and in various publications, notably *Harper's Bazaar.*

Beginning in 1951, Model taught photography for some 30 years at the New School for Social Research and, for part of that period, in private classes held at her home. Her uncompromising and passionate approach to photography influenced a

Elderly woman seated on a chair along the street on the French Riviera, photograph by Lisette Model, 1934.

great many of her students, among them Diane Arbus and Rosalind Solomon.

DIANE ARBUS

Diane Arbus (1923–1971) was the daughter of two proprietors of a department store. At age 18 she married Allan Arbus, an employee at her family's store. Before separating, they worked collaboratively, first taking photographs and creating advertisements for the store, then creating commercial fashion photography for prominent magazines of the time.

After taking a brief photography course with Berenice Abbott, Arbus met Lisette Model, an Austrian-born documentary photographer, and studied with her. With Model's encouragement Arbus gave up commercial work to concentrate on fine-art photography. In 1960 *Esquire* published Arbus's first photo-essay, in which she effectively juxtaposed privilege and squalor in New York City. Thereafter she made a living as a freelance photographer and photography instructor.

In 1963 and 1966 Arbus received Guggenheim fellowships to be part of a project titled "American Rites, Manners, and Customs." During this period she mastered her technique of using a square format, which emphasizes the subject more than the photograph's composition. She also used flash lighting, which gives her work a sense of theatricality and surrealism. She began at that time to explore the subjects that would occupy her for much of her career: individuals living on the outskirts of society and "normalcy," such as nudists, transvestites, dwarfs, and the mentally or physically handicapped. Her own evident intimacy with the extraordinary subjects of her photos resulted in images that engage the sympathy and collusion of the viewer and elicit a strong response. Some critics saw her work as remarkably empathetic to its subjects, while others were disturbed by what they saw as a harsh, voyeuristic look into the lives of the disadvantaged.

In 1971 Arbus committed suicide. A collection of her photos was published in 1972 in connection with a successful major exhibition of her work at the Museum of Modern Art in New York City. That same year her work was shown at the Venice Biennale, marking the first time that an American photographer received that distinction. In 2007 Arbus's estate gifted her complete archives—including photographic equipment, diary pages, and the negatives of some 7,500 rolls of film—to the Metropolitan Museum of Art in New York City.

MARY ELLEN MARK

Mary Ellen Mark (1940–2015) is an American photojournalist whose compelling, empathetic images document the lives of marginalized people in the United States and other countries. Born in 1940, Mark graduated from the University of Pennsylvania in Philadelphia in 1962 with a bachelor's degree in painting and art history, and in 1964 she earned a master's degree in photojournalism from the same institution. In 1974 she published her first book, *Passport*, a selection of her photographs taken from 1963 to 1973.

Mark began one of her best-known projects in 1976. For two months she lived in a high-security women's ward at the Oregon State Mental Institution in order to capture on film the moods and ongoing anxieties of mentally ill women confined to a locked ward. The resulting black-and-white images illustrate Mark's attempts to record the human condition with both compassion and objectivity.

Mark traveled repeatedly to India. On her first trip, in 1968, and then again in 1980 and 1981, she photographed Bombay's prostitutes and the work of Mother Teresa and her associates. In 1982 Mark completed an award-winning photo-essay for *Life* magazine documenting the lives of runaway children on the streets of Seattle, Washington. She later returned to Seattle to work on *Streetwise* (1984), a powerful documentary motion picture about Seattle's homeless children. She presented portraits of New York City's homeless people in the book *A Cry for Help: Stories of Homelessness and Hope* (1996).

CARRIE MAE WEEMS

Carrie Mae Weems (1953–) is an American artist and photographer known for creating installations that combine photography, audio, and text to examine many facets of contemporary American life.

Weems, who is probably best known as a photographer, initially studied modern dance. She received her first camera at age 21. In 1978 she began her first photographic project, called *Environmental Profits*, which focused on life in Portland. That same year she started her first major series, *Family Pictures and Stories*, completed about five years later. In 1981 she graduated with a B.A. from the California Institute of the Arts, and she later obtained an M.F.A. (1984) from the University of California, San Diego, and an M.A. (1987) from the University of California, Berkeley.

Weems was influenced by the work of earlier African American photographers who documented the black experience, notably Roy DeCarava. She began to refer to herself as the "image maker." Weems's early images explored personal and familial themes, as reflected in the title she used for several works, *The Kitchen Table Series* (1990). These images often were accompanied by text and audio recordings. As her work developed, she became more explicitly political, continuing to explore themes of racism and the African American experience while addressing gender issues and the nature of male-female relationships. Weems taught photography at several colleges and exhibited her works frequently. In the late 1990s and the 2000s she also embraced video technology, though the still image remained central in her work.

In 2013 Weems was named a MacArthur Foundation fellow.

SEBASTIÃO SALGADO

Sebastião Salgado, born in Brazil in 1944, is a photojournalist whose work powerfully expresses the suffering of the homeless and downtrodden. While working as an economist for the Ministry of Finance in the late 1960s, he joined the popular movement against Brazil's military government. Seen as a political radical, Salgado was exiled and fled to France. In 1971, while on an assignment in Rwanda as an economist for the International Coffee Organization, he took his first photographs and soon decided to teach himself the craft. He became a freelance photojournalist in 1973.

Over the next decade Salgado photographed a wide variety of subjects, including the famine in Niger and the civil war in Mozambique. In 1979 he joined the prestigious Magnum Photos cooperative for photojournalists, and two years later he gained prominence in the United States with a riveting photograph that captured John Hinckley's attempt to assassinate President Ronald Reagan. By the mid-1980s Salgado had begun to devote himself almost entirely to long-term projects that told a story through a series of images. By this time he also established his style: impassioned photographs grounded in great formal beauty and strong compositions, which lend a sense of nobility to his often downtrodden subjects, including Latin American peasants, African famine sufferers, and Brazilian miners.

RICHARD AVEDON

Richard Avedon (1923–2004) was one of the leading mid-20th-century photographers, noted for his portraits and fashion photographs. Avedon began to explore photography on his own at age 10 and was immediately drawn to portraiture. His first sitter was the Russian pianist-composer Sergey Rachmaninoff, who then lived in the same New York City apartment building as Avedon's grandparents. Avedon studied photography in the U.S. merchant marine, where he took identification card pictures, and at the New School for Social Research. He turned professional in 1945 and became a regular contributor to *Harper's Bazaar* and *Vogue*, in addition to working on many advertising campaigns. In 1992 he became the first staff photographer at *The New Yorker.*

Avedon's fashion photographs are characterized by a strong black-and-white contrast that creates an effect of austere sophistication. In his portraits of celebrities and other sitters, he created a sense of drama by often using a stark, white background and eliciting a frontal, confrontational pose.

Avedon's photographs are collected in several books. He also served as visual consultant for the motion picture *Funny Face* (1957), which was based on his own experiences. The Whitney Museum of American Art in New York City mounted a retrospective exhibition of Avedon's photographs in 1994.

ROBERT MAPPLETHORPE

After experimenting with underground film-making in the late 1960s, by 1970 Robert Mapplethorpe (1946–1989) was creating photographs using a Polaroid camera, often arranging them into collages or showing them as series. By the mid-1970s he received critical attention for his elegant black-and-white photographs. He experimented with different techniques, including using a large-format press camera, combining photographic images printed on linen, and designing his own wooden frames.

During this period he pursued what were to remain his favourite subjects throughout his career: still lifes, flowers, portraits of friends and celebrities (such as poet and singer Patti Smith), and homoerotic explorations of the male body. His compositions were generally stark, his combination of cold studio light and precise focus creating dramatic tonal contrasts. While these effects rendered still lifes with an almost Vermeer-like coolness, these same techniques rendered homosexual imagery in a manner that some found shocking. His muscular male models were generally framed against plain backdrops, sometimes engaged in sexual activity or posed with sadomasochistic props such as leather and chains. His clear, unflinching style challenged viewers to confront this imagery. Moreover, the combination of his choice of subject matter with the photographs' formal beauty and grounding in art-historical traditions created what many saw as a tension between pornography and art.

Mapplethorpe's reputation grew in the 1980s, and he began to focus more on flowers and celebrity portraits than on the overtly sexual subject matter of his earlier output. Still, Mapplethorpe managed to impart a sensual energy to the folds of one of his favourite subjects, the calla lily, that many would argue equalled the impact of his nudes. His work was exhibited internationally, with major shows at the Whitney Museum of American Art in New York City and the National Portrait Gallery in London. When he contracted the AIDS virus,

Mapplethorpe chronicled his illness in a harrowing series of self-portraits.

A 1990 posthumous retrospective exhibition, "Robert Mapplethorpe: The Perfect Moment," stirred a political debate. Because the exhibition—which featured Mapplethorpe's still lifes as well as his nudes—was partly funded by a grant from the National Endowment for the Arts (NEA), the exhibit sparked a debate about government subsidies of "obscene" art and provoked Congress to enact restrictions on future NEA grants. Despite of, or perhaps because of, the controversy, Mapplethorpe's reptuation as one of his era's most talented—and most provocative—photographers continued to rise.

HELEN LEVITT

Helen Levitt (1913–2009) was an American photographer whose work captures the bustle, squalor, and beauty of everyday life in New York City. At 18 she began working in a portrait studio in the Bronx. After seeing the works of French photographer Henri-Cartier Bresson, she was inspired to purchase a 35-mm Leica camera and began to scour the poor neighbourhoods of New York for subject matter. About 1938 she took her portfolio to photographer Walker Evans's studio, where she also met novelist and film critic James Agee. She struck up friendships with the two men, occasionally accompanying the former on his photo shoots in the city.

During this period Levitt often chose children, especially the underprivileged, as her subject matter. Her first show, "Photographs of Children," was held at the Museum of Modern Art in New York in 1943 and featured the humanity that infuses much of her work. Included in this show were photographs from her visit in 1941 to Mexico City, where she photographed the city's street life.

In the mid-1940s Levitt collaborated with Agee, filmmaker Sidney Meyers, and painter Janice Loeb on *The Quiet One*, a prizewinning documentary about a young African American boy, and with Agee and Loeb on the film *In the Street*, which captures everyday life in East Harlem. For the next decade she concentrated on film editing and directing. In 1959 and 1960 she received Guggenheim Fellowships to investigate techniques using colour photography. The slides that resulted from the project, shown at the Museum of Modern Art in New York in 1963, were stolen from her apartment before they could be duplicated. Levitt focused for the rest of the 1960s on film work and resumed photography in the 1970s, with a major Museum of Modern Art show in 1974.

CINDY SHERMAN

Cindy Sherman (1954–) started as a painter but switched to photography while still in college. After graduation, she began work on *Untitled Film Stills* (1977–80), one of her best-known series. The series of 8 x 10-inch (20 x 25cm) black-and-white photographs featuring Sherman in a variety of roles is reminiscent of film noir and presents viewers with an ambiguous portrayal of women as sex objects. Sherman stated that the series was "about the fakeness of role-playing as well as contempt for the domineering 'male' audience who would mistakenly read the images as sexy." She continued to be the model in her photographs, donning wigs and costumes that evoke images from the realms of advertising, television, film, and fashion and that, in turn, challenge the cultural stereotypes supported by these media.

During the 1980s Sherman began to use colour film, to exhibit very large prints, and to concentrate more on lighting and facial expression. Using prosthetic appendages and liberal amounts of makeup, Sherman moved into the realm of the grotesque and the sinister with photographs that featured mutilated bodies and reflected such concerns as eating disorders, insanity, and death. Her work became less ambiguous, focusing perhaps more on the result of society's acceptance of stereotyped roles for women than upon the roles themselves.

Sherman returned to ironic commentary upon clichéd female identities in the 1990s, introducing mannequins into some of her photographs, and in 1997 she directed the dark comedic film *Office Killer*. Two years later she exhibited disturbing images of savaged dolls and doll parts that explored her interest in juxtaposing violence and artificiality. Sherman continued these juxtapositions in a 2000 series of photographs in which she posed as Hollywood women with overblown makeup and silicone breast implants, again achieving a result of enigmatic pathos. A 2012 retrospective at the Museum of Modern Art (MoMA) in New York City was accompanied by a film series comprising movies that Sherman saw as having influenced her work.

ANNIE LEIBOVITZ

Born in Connecticut in 1949, Annie Leibovitz grew up the daughter of a military father. The family was living in the Philippines in 1967 when Leibovitz enrolled in the San Francisco Art Institute, intending to become a painter. After taking a night class in photography, she quickly became engrossed in that medium. In 1970, while still a student, she was given her first commercial assignment for *Rolling Stone* magazine: to photograph John Lennon. Three years later Leibovitz became the publication's chief photographer, directing her energies toward a unique presentation of the major personalities of contemporary rock music. In 1975 she documented the Rolling Stones' six-month North American concert tour, during which she shot several widely reproduced photographs of guitarist Keith Richards and lead singer Mick Jagger. (She also became addicted to cocaine, a habit she kicked some years later when she joined the staff of *Vanity Fair* magazine.) Perhaps her most famous work from this period is a portrait of Lennon and Yoko Ono that was published on the cover of *Rolling Stone* in January 1981. In the picture, shot mere hours before Lennon's assassination, the singer-songwriter is nude and wrapped fetuslike around his fully clothed wife.

In 1983 Leibovitz produced a 60-print show that toured Europe and the United States. That same year she joined the staff of *Vanity Fair*, which broadened her pool of subjects to include film stars, athletes, and political figures. For her portraits, Leibovitz—who viewed her photographic sessions as collaborations—typically spent days observing her subjects' daily lives and worked to make her portraits of them unique and witty, each a technically exquisite distillation. Her commercial images were dramatic and staged rather than casual.

She received the American Society of Magazine Photographers award for photographer of the year in 1983. She began to work as an advertising photographer in 1986. Her style

Celebrity portraitist Annie Leibovitz photographs singer Jennifer

throughout these projects was characterized by carefully staged settings, superb lighting, and her trademark use of vivid colour.

In 1991 Leibovitz had her first museum exhibition; she became the first woman and second living photographer to show at the National Portrait Gallery in Washington, D.C. She also earned much praise for her portraits of American Olympians taken for an exhibit at the 1996 Summer Games in Atlanta, Georgia.

In 2000 Leibovitz was among the first group of Americans to be designated a Library of Congress Living Legend. Leibovitz's perfectionism in her work (budgets were exploded, and no expense was spared) and her celebrity-touched lifestyle had a role in producing a debt of $24 million, for which she was sued in 2009. The suit against her was settled, and the glare of publicity was deflected somewhat when her official portrait of the first family— Pres. Barack Obama, his wife, Michelle, and his daughters, Sasha and Malia—was released to the public later that year. The photographer's achievements were celebrated in *Annie Leibovitz: Life Through a Lens* (2009), a documentary film made for public television's *American Masters* series by her sister Barbara. During her financial difficulties, Leibovitz began working on a personal project, photographing places and objects that were meaningful to her.

As a means of visual communication and expression, photography has distinct aesthetic capabilities. The essential elements of the photographic image are usually established immediately at the time of exposure. This characteristic is unique to photography and sets it apart from other ways of picture making. The seemingly automatic recording of an image by photography has given the process a sense of authenticity shared by no other picture-making technique. The photograph possesses, in the popular mind, such apparent accuracy that the adage "the camera does not lie" has become an accepted, if erroneous, cliché.

This understanding of photography's supposed objectivity has dominated evaluations of its role in the arts. In the early part of its history, photography was sometimes belittled as a mechanical art because of its dependence on technology. In truth, however, photography is not the automatic process that is implied by the use of a camera. Although the camera usually limits the photographer to depicting existing objects rather than imaginary or interpretive views, the skilled photographer can introduce creativity into the process.

He or she chooses the vantage point and the exact moment of exposure. The

photographer perceives the essential qualities of the subject and interprets it according
to his or her judgment, taste, and involvement.
An effective photograph can disseminate
information about humanity and nature,
record the visible world, and extend human
knowledge and understanding. For all these
reasons, photography has aptly been called
the most important invention since the printing press.

GLOSSARY

abstract Expressing ideas and emotions by using elements such as colors and lines without attempting to create a realistic picture.

aesthetic Having to do with beauty or with what is beautiful.

albumen paper Light-sensitive paper prepared by coating with albumen, or egg white, and a salt (e.g., ammonium chloride) and sensitized by an aftertreatment with a solution of silver nitrate.

aperture An opening that controls the amount of light that passes through a camera lens.

avant-garde A group of people who develop new and often very surprising ideas in the arts.

calotype Early photographic technique by which a large number of prints could be produced from a paper negative.

camera lucida An optical instrument patented in 1806 by William Hyde Wollaston to facilitate accurate sketching of objects.

camera obscura A darkened enclosure having an aperture usually provided with a lens through which light from external objects enters to form an image of the objects on the opposite surface.

caricature An artistic representation that has the qualities of caricature.

carte-de-visite A calling card, especially one with a photographic portrait mounted on it.

chronophotography A photograph or a series of photographs of a moving object taken to record and exhibit successive phases of the object's motion.

daguerreotype An early photograph produced on a silver or a silver-covered copper plate.

heliograph An apparatus for telegraphing by means of the sun's rays flashed from a mirror.

ideologue An impractical idealist.

landscape A picture of natural inland scenery.

photojournalism Journalism in which written copy is subordinate to pictorial, usually photographic, presentation of news stories.

Pictorialism A movement or technique in photography emphasizing artificial, often romanticized, pictorial qualities.

portraiture Portraits of people.

Precisionism A movement in photography characterized by sharply defined imagery, especially of objects removed from their actual context.

shutter A device through which the lens aperture of a camera is opened to admit light and thus expose the film (or the electronic image sensor of a digital camera).

stereoscopic photography Two-dimensional photographs that when viewed by both eyes appear to exist in three dimensions in space.

street photography A genre that records everyday life in a public place. The very publicness of the setting enables the photographer to take candid pictures of strangers, often without their knowledge.

tintype A positive photograph produced by applying a collodion-nitrocellulose solution to a thin, black-enameled metal plate immediately before exposure.

wet collodion process A technique for making glass negatives using a solution of nitrocellulose (guncotton) in alcohol and ether.

BIBLIOGRAPHY

Early historical overviews of the development of the art of photography are provided in Robert Taft, *Photography and the American Scene: A Social History, 1839–1889* (1938, reprinted 1964); Helmut Gernsheim, *Creative Photography: Aesthetic Trends, 1839–1960*, rev. and updated (1962, reprinted 1991); Michel F. Braive, *The Era of the Photograph: A Social History*, trans. by David Britt (1966; originally published in French, 1965); and Peter Pollack, *The Picture History of Photography: From the Earliest Beginnings to the Present Day* (1958, reissued 1977), especially valuable for its wealth of illustrations. Other titles include William Welling, *Photography in America: The Formative Years, 1839–1900* (1978, reprinted 1987); Petr Tausk, *Photography in the 20th Century*, trans. by Veronica Talbot and J. David Beal (1980; originally published in German, 1977); Beaumont Newhall, *The History of Photography: From 1839 to the Present*, rev. and enlarged, 5th ed. (1982, reissued 1999), which examines the stylistic development of the art of photography as related to the technological and scientific characteristics of the medium; Helmut Gernsheim, *The History of Photography*, rev. 3rd ed., 2 vol. (1982; vol. 2 reissued 1988); Peter Turner (ed.), *American Images: Photography 1945–1980* (1985); Jean-Claude Lemagny and André Rouillé (eds.), *A History of Photog-*

raphy: Social and Cultural Perspectives, trans. by Janet Lloyd (1987; originally published in French, 1986); John Wade, *The Camera from the 11th Century to the Present Day* (1990); Martha A. Sandweiss (ed.), *Photography in 19th Century America* (1991); Heinz K. Henisch and Bridget A. Henisch, *The Photographic Experience, 1839–1914: Images and Attitudes* (1994); Naomi Rosenblum, *A World History of Photography*, 3rd ed. (1997); Michel Frizot (ed.), *New History of Photography* (1998, originally published in French, 1994); Keith F. Davis, *An American Century of Photography: From Dry-Plate to Digital*, 2nd ed., rev. and enlarged (1999); and Naomi Rosenblum, *A History of Women Photographers*, 2nd ed. updated and expanded (2000).

Studies of particular schools and types of photography include Richard Rudisill, *Mirror Image: The Influence of the Daguerreotype on American Society* (1971), a thorough survey; Beaumont Newhall, *The Daguerreotype in America*, 3rd rev. ed. (1976), a study of the industry as well as the art of daguerreotyping; Robert Doty, *Photo Secession: Photography as a Fine Art* (1960; also published as *Photo-Secession: Stieglitz and the Fine-Art Movement in Photography*, 1978), an account of events leading up to and following the founding of the society by Alfred Stieglitz; Marianne Fulton (ed.), Bonnie Yochelson, and Kathleen A. Erwin, *Pictorialism into Modernism: The Clarence H. White School of Photography* (1996); Margaret Harker, *The Linked Ring: The Secession Movement in Photography in Britain, 1892–1910* (1979); William Culp Darrah, *Stereo Views: A History of Stereographs in America and Their Collection* (1964); Ben Maddow, Faces: *A Narrative History of the Portrait in Photography*, ed. and comp. by Constance Sullivan (1977); Van Deren Coke, *Avant-Garde Photography in Germany, 1919–1939*, trans. from German (1982); Rainer Fabian and Hans-Christian Adam, *Masters of Early Travel Photography* (1983; originally published in German, 1981); *Bauhaus Photography* (1985; originally published in German, Roswitha Fricke (ed.), 1982); and Tina Ruisinger, *Faces of Photography: Encounters with 50 Master Photographers of the 20th Century* (2002).

INDEX